The Word Explained

. . . .

A Homily for Every Sunday of the Year

Year B

William J. Byron, SJ

Paulist Press
New York / Mahwah, NJ

Cover image: Background art by Eky Studio / Shutterstock.com. All rights reserved.
Cover design by Sharyn Banks
Book design by Lynn Else

Library of Congress Control Number: 2014952201

ISBN 978-0-8091-4811-0 (paperback)
ISBN 978-1-58768-447-0 (e-book)

Published by Paulist Press
997 Macarthur Boulevard
Mahwah, New Jersey 07430

www.paulistpress.com

Printed and bound in the
United States of America

Contents

CONTENTS

CONTENTS

To the Sunday worshipping community
at the Chapel of Saint Joseph's University,
Philadelphia, PA,
and at
Annunciation of the Blessed Virgin Mary Parish,
Havertown, PA

Introduction

This, as I said in the introduction to *The Word Proclaimed* (the first volume in a set of three), is a book without a theme, unless the liturgical calendar can be said to provide a seasons-of-the-year theme for the Sunday homily. It is, however, a book based on a theory—a theory of the homily—namely, that every homily should be an extension of the proclamation. This is the liturgical principle that underlies every chapter in this book and its two companion volumes that complete the coverage of Years A, B, and C of readings in the Sunday lectionary.

Sacred Scripture from the Old and New Testaments is proclaimed in the first part of every eucharistic liturgy. The homilist then extends the proclamation by filtering it through his or her own faith experience and tries to match it up with the faith experience of the people in the pews. That is always a challenge; but being mindful of the challenge to extend the proclamation in this way provides the homilist with direction in rendering this service to the people of God. Homilists have a personal responsibility to heed and incorporate into their own style of delivery these words from the pen of St. Augustine: "[I]f I speak to someone without feeling, he does not understand what I am saying" (from a *Treatise on John*, Tract 26).

We are a Sunday people, we Catholic Christians. We gather in eucharistic assemblies every Sunday to remember the Lord in the breaking of the bread. In this way we give praise and thanks to God. That is our Sunday obligation—to give thanks to God. We thus declare ourselves to be "much obliged"—to be grateful and we express that gratitude in praise of God and love of neighbor. Gratitude is the foundation of our religious observance. It is in gratitude that we gather to hear the word and share in the breaking of the bread. Nourished every Sunday by both word and sacrament, we go forth each week to serve our neighbor.

We break open the Scriptures in our Sunday assemblies where we find Christ present not only in (1) the eucharistic elements, (2) the faithful who are gathered there, and (3) the person of the priest-presider, but also in (4) the proclamation of the word and the accompanying homily. A well-prepared homily is filtered first through the faith experience of the homilist and, so far as possible, matched up to meet the faith experience of the faithful in the pews. Somehow Christ is there in both pulpit and pew.

This book is a collection of one homilist's efforts to extend the proclamation in ways that will touch the hearts and minds of believers. Every chapter in this book is a delivered homily. They've been road-tested in parishes and university chapels. They've been preached, heard, reflected upon, and discussed. Standing alone as a book, apart from any liturgical setting, this collection might prove helpful (if taken just one homily at a time) to the people who belong to any parish community. On the desks of priests and deacons, this book could serve as a source of ideas for extending the proclamation and matching it to the faith experience of those the homilists are privileged to serve.

To the extent that this book proves useful to the occupant of any pulpit or pew, or to any reader interested in reflecting on God's word in quiet moments apart from the crowd, my purpose in putting it together will have been achieved.

I've heard it remarked recently by a disaffected and discouraged Catholic worshipper that in the United States we have "*Saturday Night Live* and Sunday morning dead." I hope this book can help to change that. I've also heard from a pastor who hosted a foreign pastor during a visit to this country that his guest commented to him: "I notice that in your churches the benches and kneelers have cushions; I've noticed that your homilies are usually cushioned too." Perhaps the to-the-point style of the homilies offered here will facilitate the discovery of both challenge and encouragement in the word proclaimed, the word explained, and the word received.

—W.J.B.

I
Advent

. . . .

1

First Sunday of Advent

Isaiah 63:16–17, 19; 64:2–7; Psalm 80;
1 Corinthians 1:3–9; Mark 13:33–37

WHY DO YOU LET US WANDER, O LORD?

Isaiah raises a good question for your consideration on this the First Sunday of Advent. He asks, "Why do you let us wander, O Lord?"

The immediate answer to that question is: Because you are free—free, quite literally, to do what you want to do with your life, with your time, your treasure, your talents. You are free to use your freedom well or badly. You can wander all you want. Since that is indeed the case, you can come to appreciate the fact that Advent is a time to check to see where that wandering is getting you.

You might hear the Lord saying to you this morning: How's it going? How is your wandering progressing? Are you moving forward or in circles? Are you targeted onto anything of real significance? Are you aiming high, or low, or nowhere in particular? Is yours a purpose-driven life?

And Isaiah, who raised this issue for you today in the first place, prefaced his question with the assertion: "You, Lord, are our father." And toward the end of today's Advent reading from Isaiah, the Prophet repeats the assertion, "Yet, Lord, you are our father"—as if to say, despite our wanderings you are still our father. And given our wanderings, Isaiah seems to be saying, perhaps you, Father, are falling down on your job; you haven't been holding us in check. Isaiah then leaves you with a familiar image by speaking to the Lord in these words: "[W]e are the clay and you are the potter: we are all the work of your hands."

We don't ordinarily think of ourselves as clay, although we know that we were once dry clay—dust—"and unto dust" we shall return.

Stay with that image of potter and clay for awhile today. God, our creator, is like a potter. He can shape us, form us, spin us on his potter's wheel. But he is a highly unusual potter in giving life and freedom to his clay—freedom of thought, freedom of movement, freedom of choice, freedom of will and the ability to do what is good or what is evil.

Isaiah, you will remember, seems to be complaining that the potter let the clay splatter a bit and run off the wheel: "Why do you let us wander, O Lord, from your ways and harden our hearts so that we fear you not?"

Again, consider the question of human freedom and divine foreknowledge; the mystery of an all-powerful, all-loving God content to sit back, so to speak, and observe our wanderings, watch us use our freedom badly.

I cannot solve that problem for you now—the question of divine foreknowledge and human freedom. Divine power and foreknowledge means that God, on the one hand, has to be something more than an observer and puppet master, and we humans, on the other hand, gifted as we are with free will, have to be something more than puppets on a string. Let me simply suggest that Advent is a time to look into our wanderings, to check up on the extent to which we are using our freedom wisely, to examine how close we may have come to breaking that string or tying it all up into knots.

"Lord, make us turn to you," you said repeatedly in the Responsorial Psalm. Yet you know he will not "make" you do anything. You are free. You have to choose. You have to decide. You have to decide to turn toward God. The invitation is there. God's grace is there drawing you toward him. But you have to choose. You have to decide to make that turn quite literally a conversion—a turning toward God. He is waiting. You'll be welcome; you know that. Advent is the time to think about going out to greet him when he comes.

The Church, rather generously, it seems to me, applies St. Paul's words from First Corinthians—you heard them in the second reading today—to each one of us. Paul speaks of the "grace of God bestowed on you in Christ Jesus, that in whom you were enriched in every way, with all discourse and all knowledge."

And the Gospel reading from Mark, short and to the point, levels with you. Mark has Jesus say to you: "Be watchful! Be alert! You do not know when the time will come. . . . What I say to you, I say to all: 'Watch!'"

Well, there you have it, my dear friends, my fellow wanderers. You might call it an Advent warning; or you can think of it as an Advent invitation. Advent is the time to get your clay together and to take greater care to make sure that the exercise of your freedom is where both you and God want it to be—in the hands of your Father, your Lord, who speaks to you today through these wonderful Advent readings.

2

Second Sunday of Advent

Isaiah 40:1–5, 9–11; Psalm 85; 2 Peter 3:8–14; Mark 1:1–8

PREPARE THE WAY OF THE LORD

On this, the Second Sunday of Advent, we meet John the Baptist, a strong and central figure in our Advent liturgies. John, as Mark's Gospel describes him, "was clothed in camel's hair, with a leather belt around his waist. He fed on locusts and wild honey."

Meet John the Baptizer once again at this hour. Hear him proclaim to you an Advent message taken from the Prophet Isaiah: "Prepare the way of the Lord! Make straight his paths!" That's what John the Baptist did. That's what the Church invites each one of us to consider doing now.

If it helps, let background music from Handel's *Messiah* roll around in your memory: "Every valley shall be filled in, every mountain and hill shall be made low. . . . The glory of the Lord shall be revealed, and all the people shall see it together." Isaiah's words. Handel's music. John the Baptizer's prophetic message: "Prepare the way of the Lord!"

With or without music, think of this world—our world—as you know it. Think of the valleys that need filling in—valleys of despair, hopelessness, hunger, homelessness. Think of those valleys that take the form of income gaps, the needs single mothers have for daycare, health care, transportation, and training; think of educational deficits, discounted life expectancies, lowered immune systems, joblessness, loneliness, and all the other valleys that swallow human dignity and human hope. Preparing the way of the Lord in our world today means doing what we can to fill those valleys in, and to convert our modern wastelands into a highway for our God.

It was back on May 9, 1961, when Newton Minow made his famous wasteland comment about television in a speech to the National Association of Broadcasters. Listen to Newton Minow speaking in 1961:

> I invite you to sit down in front of your television set when your station goes on the air and stay there without a book, magazine, newspaper, profit-and-loss sheet or rating book to distract you—and keep your eyes glued to that set until the station signs off. I can assure you that you will observe a vast wasteland.
>
> You will see a procession of game shows, violence, audience-participation shows, formula comedies about totally unbelievable families, blood and thunder, mayhem, violence, sadism, murder, western bad men, western good men, private eyes, gangsters, more violence and cartoons. And, endlessly, commercials—many screaming, cajoling and offending. And most of all, boredom. True, you will see a few things you will enjoy. But they will be very, very few. And if you think I exaggerate, try it.

That was 1961. Arguably, things are worse today in a never-sign-off TV land made vaster by cable, and in the new wasteland world of Internet imagery. The point of all this is not to beat up on television producers or Internet service providers. It is simply to point out to you that there are valleys there that need filling in with new ideas, beautiful images, and creative programming by those in a position to shape the media into a welcoming road for the coming of the Lord. The Lord wants to come again this Christmas to a waiting world that is weighted, burdened with need, over-weighted, in fact, with need for beauty, love, justice, and peace—all that Advent promises. What can you do to meet that need? Think about it today. Each one of us can do something on the job, at home, or as a volunteer.

"Every mountain and hill shall be made low," proclaimed Isaiah and John the Baptist echoed him. We've got work to do. Think about climbing that mountain to peace in the Middle East. Think about knocking down the hills and mountains of racism all around us. Think of what might be done to lower the mountains of greed in the economy, addiction in both slums and suburbs, violence in families and schools, and think about lowering those hills that block meaningful communication in families, between spouses, as well as between parents and their off-spring. Lowering all of these is an important way of preparing the way of the Lord. We've got work to do this Advent.

And if you need a bit of a lift in the face of the mounting obstacles to the coming of Christ in the world that you inhabit every day, turn again to our second reading, the selection from the Second Letter of Peter, who reminds you that your Lord "is patient with you, not wishing that any should perish but that all should come to repentance." Try it. Repentance means an attitudinal turnaround, a value reversal, a change of heart so that your will is aligned with the will of God.

And Peter goes on to ask: "What sort of persons ought you to be?" He answers by saying you should be "conducting yourselves in holiness and devotion, waiting for and hastening the coming of the day of God." You can't be content to just wait. You've got to do what you can to "hasten" the coming of God's promised justice, love, and peace.

So, get to work, dear friends. It is Advent—a time to make sure that you are busy about the right things.

3

Third Sunday of Advent

Isaiah 61:1–2a, 10–11; Luke 1:46–54;
1 Thessalonians 5:16–24; John 1:6–8, 19–28

BROTHERS AND SISTERS: REJOICE!

Rejoice! Gaudete! Be happy! This is Gaudete Sunday, the Third Sunday of Advent. It's called "Gaudete" because that imperative verb was the first word in the Introit, the introductory verse of the old Latin Mass on this third Sunday of Advent for many centuries. It is there in the opening of the second reading today. It comes from Paul's First Letter to the Thessalonians, the fifth chapter: "Rejoice always!"

That's an order, a command. Rejoice! Gaudete! Be happy on this Third Sunday of Advent. Rejoice in anticipation of the coming of Christ to you, directly to you, to your heart again this year at Christmas.

This is why pink vestments are worn today. This is why the third of the four Advent-wreath candles is pink, not the darker purple color of the other three candles. The color pink is lighter, as is the mood presumably of the worshipper, on this the Third Sunday of Advent.

Here at Holy Trinity, this 5:30 Sunday Mass is well known and much appreciated for being bright, light-hearted, and vibrant; this liturgy is always a "gaudete" celebration. Mary Lou Galvin gives the imperative command; she orders all of you: Rejoice! Be happy! Sing out strong from a deep faith and a happy heart! Gaudete!

You may be surprised to learn that there is a journal of happiness. It is an academic journal edited in the United States and printed in the Netherlands: *The Journal of Happiness*. You can find it on the Web. "What Makes for a Merry Christmas?" is the title of a recent article. If you had been commissioned to write that article, what do you think your answer to this question might be: "What Makes for a Merry Christmas?"

The article in the *Journal of Happiness* begins by identifying the different types of activities and experiences that people associate with Christmas and tries to measure the relative impact of each experience category on happiness, on a general feeling of well-being. The experience areas are well known to you all: (1) Spending time with family; (2) Participating in religious activities; (3) Maintaining traditions (like decorating a Christmas tree); (4) Spending money on others via the purchase of gifts; (5) Receiving gifts from others; (6) Helping others; and (7) Enjoying the sensual aspects of the holiday (for example, good food). The researchers concluded "that family and religion provided the greatest benefit to holiday well-being, whereas the secular, materialistic aspects of the holiday either contributed little to Christmas joy, or were associated with less happiness and more stress and unpleasant affect." No great surprise there. The article closes with these words: "[T]he path to a merry Christmas comes not from purchasing many expensive gifts at the mall, wrapping them, and placing them under the tree, but instead from satisfying deeper needs to be close to one's family and find meaning in life."

Ah, but there, for some, lies the rub. Family relations may be in need of repair. Life may—because of personal failure, job loss, physical illness, loss of a loved one—seem devoid of meaning.

I'll come back to that important point in a minute, but first let me suggest that because materialism can mar our gift giving and getting, it might be profitable to reflect for a moment on the true story of the enduring romance, despite some bumps on their marital road, between journalist playwright Charles MacArthur and his wife, the great actress Helen Hayes. You elders will remember her as the "first lady of the American theater." When they were young and engaged to be married, Charles MacArthur bought Helen Hayes a bag of peanuts one day, presented them with a flourish, and said: "I wish they were emeralds." Years later, as he was dying, he gave his wife an emerald bracelet and said, "I wish they were peanuts." To a great extent your happiness at this time of year depends on your ability to keep the value of peanut experiences and emerald experiences in perspective.

And you all know the famous O. Henry story, "The Gift of the Magi." The young wife Della is depressed and frantic at Christmastime because she has just a dollar or two to use to buy a gift for her husband Jim, who is also financially strapped and saddened because he cannot afford an expensive gift for her.

Della has long, beautiful hair and decides to sell it to a wig-maker in order to get enough money to buy for Jim a platinum fob chain to adorn his one prized possession, a handsome gold pocket watch that belonged to his father and grandfather before him. And Jim, as those of you who know the story will recall, decides on Christmas Eve to sell the watch in order to be able to buy an expensive set of pure tortoiseshell combs, with jeweled rims, to give to Della to adorn her beautiful hair.

When they exchanged their gifts on Christmas Eve—beautiful combs for her who had sold her hair; a handsome watch fob for him who had pawned his watch—they suddenly realized that the gifts were unimportant. The only thing of any consequence was their love for one another.

Rejoice! Gaudete! Be happy! Are you ready for that, even if family relations may be in need of repair and your life may seem to be devoid of meaning? Are you looking for happiness in the right places? It may sound self-serving or self-interested for me to say that you are in the right place right now to look for happiness. You can find it in this community, in the eucharistic Prayer that will be said at the altar in just a few moments, in the songs you sing here, in the sacrament you share with others throughout the world in the body and blood of Christ—your meal at this table. You are looking in the right place when you look for happiness right here. Perhaps your conscience is suggesting that you should look to those confessional doors in the back of the church. When the green light is on next Saturday afternoon, open that door, walk in, unburden yourself, be reconciled with God, and experience the happiness of reconciliation.

Each one of us is engaged in a search for meaning. That search can bring you to Christ. The two of you—you and Christ—can meet as question and answer. Rejoice that your answer is at hand!

Look around you to see if there is a John the Baptist somewhere in your life, a John or Jane whose voice and example can show you the way to Jesus Christ in whom you can find joy at Christmastime, no matter what your circumstances might be, it is Jesus Christ in whom and through whom you will find joy now and gain eternal happiness, because that's the route to happiness that God wills for you.

Believe that. And listen again to St. Paul: "Brothers and sisters: Rejoice always. Pray without ceasing. In all circumstances give thanks, for this is the will of God for you in Christ Jesus." Rejoice!

4

Fourth Sunday of Advent

2 Samuel 7:1–5, 8b–12, 14a, 16; Psalm 89;
Romans 16:25–27; Luke 1:26–38

"DO NOT BE AFRAID, MARY"

Hail Mary! Ave Maria! Here we are in Luke's Gospel on this Fourth Sunday of Advent with the scriptural foundation of our universal Catholic devotion to Mary. Hail, Mary, full of grace!

I have three points for your consideration and prayerful reflection this morning—all three taken from the Gospel reading you just heard. The first: "Hail, Mary, full of grace! The Lord is with you!"

Second, "But [Mary] was greatly troubled at what was said."

And third: "Do not be afraid, Mary."

All hail to Mary who enjoyed the fullness of grace. But even Mary, full of grace, could be "troubled" at a crisis point in her young life. And there for Mary, as for you and me today, were the reassuring words from God's messenger Gabriel: "Do not be afraid."

Good thoughts as Christmas approaches. Good points to ponder. So let's turn our eyes and hearts to Mary this morning. To Mary, Mother of God; to Mary, mother of each one of us. Hail, Mary; it is good for us to be in touch with you!

When some people hear the words "Hail, Mary," they think of a penance assigned after confession, or a desperation pass in a football game. But today let all of us think of Mary as friend, mother, intercessor, understanding advocate, patient listener, resourceful provider for all of us, her children.

Hail, Mary! You really are wonderful, special, unique. Because God, from all eternity, decided that you would be the mother of Jesus, you were conceived free of original sin, free of the inherited guilt that all of us received as a result of the sin, original sin, of our first parents Adam and Eve. You were exempt from that, Mary, because you had a special mission, and your freedom from original sin prepared you for that mission. Your exemption meant that you were "full of grace." Your mission meant that, not only did you bring Christ into the world, you brought and continue to bring us out of the darkness of sin into the light of grace and the love of Christ. You intercede for us with your Son and we, because of you, are also blessed.

That's point number one. We hail her because she is special, full of grace, and faithful to her mission of helping us. Hail, Mary, full of grace!

Point number two is a reassuring one for us, a comforting realization that even Mary, special as she was, could be troubled—"greatly troubled" as the words of this morning's Gospel put it. She was upset, a bit disoriented, as she "pondered" what the message of the angel Gabriel was all about. There she was—a fifteen- or sixteen-year-old girl—being told that she would conceive in her womb and bring forth a son who was to be named "Jesus," a name that means "Yahweh saves." This Jesus was the promised Messiah, the Savior the world was waiting for. She was understandably troubled because she didn't know how this was going to happen. She said to the angel Gabriel: "How can this be, since I have no relations with a man?" She was not naïve. She was innocent, but not ignorant. She knew the facts of life but was troubled at her expected accommodation to a dimension of life that was clearly new to her—a supernatural intervention from the living God whose "Holy Spirit," Gabriel explained, "will come upon you, and the power of the Most High will overshadow you." No wonder she was troubled!

And now consider point number three: "Do not be afraid." You have nothing to fear, Mary, "for you have found favor with God." "Favor" is another word for grace. Each one of you has found favor with God. Each one of you was graced by God in baptism. Each one of you has received more grace—the gift of God's life and love within you—in the Eucharist, in the sacrament of reconciliation, in the sacraments of confirmation and matrimony, and the sacrament of the sick if you ever received that comforting sacrament. In any and all sacraments, you receive a fuller measure of grace; not the "fullness of grace," of course, but a fuller measure. And therefore, I can say to you, as Gabriel said to Mary, "Do not be afraid . . . for you have found favor with God."

Does "Hail, Mary" make you think at all about the Rosary?

It came as a surprise to many when Garry Wills, one of the most influential Catholic intellectuals at work in the United States today, disclosed recently that he prays the Rosary every day. It was no surprise at all, of course, when Pope John Paul II told the world that the Rosary was his favorite prayer. The occasion of Wills's remark was the publication of his book, *Why I Am a Catholic* (Houghton-Mifflin). The occasion of the Holy Father's praise for the Rosary was the publication on October 16, 2002, of his apostolic letter *Rosarium Virginis Mariae* (retrievable from the Vatican Web site at www.vatican.va/holy_fat . . . /hf_jpii_apl_20021016_rosarium-virginis-mariae_en.htm).

The Rosary, wrote John Paul II, "though clearly Marian in character, is at heart a Christocentric prayer." He surprised the Catholic world by introducing a new set of mysteries to be contemplated while reciting the Rosary (more on those in a moment). "To recite the Rosary is nothing other than to contemplate with Mary the face of Christ," said John Paul II in proclaiming the twelve months from October 2002 to October 2003 to be the "Year of the Rosary." And what is the rationale for reciting the Rosary, according to Pope John Paul? "The supreme poet Dante expresses it marvelously in the lines sung by Saint Bernard: 'Lady, thou art so great and so powerful, that whoever desires grace yet does not turn to thee, would have his desire fly without wings.'" Think about that for a moment or two this morning. Don't let your desire for grace "fly without wings." Go to Mary. And one route to Mary that you may not have tried lately is the Rosary.

There were historic circumstances that prompted John Paul II to encourage the practice of the Rosary, indeed to invite all to "rediscover the Rosary in the light of Scripture, in harmony with the Liturgy, and in the context of [our] daily lives." Those circumstances were, first, the need to pray for peace in light of "the grave challenges confronting the world at the start of this new Millennium, [when] only an intervention from on high, capable of guiding the hearts of those living in situations of conflict and those governing the destinies of nations, can give reason to hope for a brighter future."

Second, there was need to restore the Rosary as "a prayer of and for the family." "Many of the problems facing contemporary families, especially in economically developed societies, result from their increasing difficulty in communicating. Families seldom manage to come together, and the rare occasions when they do are often taken up with watching television. To return to the recitation of the family rosary means filling daily life with very different images, images of the mystery of salvation."

The pope didn't say it would be easy, but he did say, and these are his own words, "Why not try it? With God's help, a pastoral approach to youth which is positive, impassioned and creative . . . is capable of achieving quite remarkable results. If the Rosary is well presented, I am sure that young people will once more surprise adults by making this prayer their own and recite it with the enthusiasm typical of their age group."

Presenting it well to the young is no small challenge.

The Rosary, as we have known it for centuries, bypasses the entire public life of Christ (who is last seen as a twelve-year-old turning up in the Temple [fifth joyful mystery] and not heard from again until contemplated in his "Agony in the Garden" [first sorrowful mystery]), Pope John Paul II introduced five new "mysteries of light," all taken from the public life of Jesus, because he wanted the Rosary to be more truly a "compendium of the Gospel."

The five new mysteries of light were chosen because they are significant and luminous moments in the public life of Christ: (1) his baptism in the Jordan; (2) his self-manifestation at the wedding in Cana; (3) his proclamation of the kingdom of God, with a concomitant call to conversion; (4) his transfiguration; and (5) his institution of the Eucharist. Each has an easily retrievable "icon" in the imagination; each has a scriptural address in the Gospel. Each is "a revelation of the Kingdom now present in the very person of Jesus."

So, dear friends, get out your rosaries and try the mysteries of light! Meanwhile, salute Mary with your prayer of praise. Recognize that she knew trouble and anxiety, just as you do. And have the courage she had to say OK to the message God wants to be delivered to you today: "Do not be afraid, Mary [or Jack, or Ellen, or George]" whatever your name might be, whatever the source of your fear today, "Do not be afraid, for you have found favor with God."

Mary's response was a bit more eloquent than a simple, "OK." You can, if you wish, make her words your own: "May it be done to me according to your word."

II
Christmas

. . . .

5

Christmas Vigil

Isaiah 62:1–5; Psalm 89; Acts 13:16–17, 22–25; Matthew 1:1–25

THROUGH THE POWER OF THE HOLY SPIRIT

Listen carefully, dear friends, to a key phrase in the Gospel reading from Matthew that is ours to reflect on during this Christmas Vigil liturgy, namely, "through the power of the Holy Spirit." You heard that phrase in this fuller context in the Gospel of Matthew this evening: "Now this is how the birth of Jesus Christ came about. When his mother Mary was engaged to Joseph, but before they lived together, she was found with child through the power of the Holy Spirit." *Through the power of the Holy Spirit.*

How did Mary become pregnant? "Through the power of the Holy Spirit." How did the great work of the salvation of the human race begin? "Through the power of the Holy Spirit." How does this work continue today? "Through the power of the Holy Spirit."

The Spirit is alive and active and in our midst this evening, just as the Spirit was alive and active at that moment centuries ago when the angel Gabriel appeared to the maiden Mary and announced to her— a Jewish teenager—that she was to become the Mother of God. You will remember that Mary was "greatly troubled" with this news and asked, "How can this be, since I have no relations with a man?" And the angel said to her in reply: "The holy Spirit will come upon you, and the power of the Most High will overshadow you."

What do you think that expression, "Holy Spirit," meant to Mary when the angel spoke those words? What or who did she understand or imagine the Holy Spirit to be? Perhaps she let her memory turn back to references to the Holy Spirit in the psalms—her daily prayer book. From Psalm 51, for example, she may have often prayed, "Do not drive me from your presence, nor take from me your holy spirit. / Restore my joy in your salvation; sustain in me a willing spirit."

Or these words from Psalm 33 may have been familiar to her: "By the Lord's word the heavens were made; / by the breath of his mouth all their host [a reference to the stars in the sky]." Mary may have thought of the Spirit as a breath, a movement in our midst; and, the reference given there in Psalm 33 that the Lord's word produced the heavens may have suggested to Mary that a creative force was associated with the presence of the Spirit in our world.

And addressing the Lord in the words of Psalm 104, Mary may often have said, "Lord my God, you are great indeed! . . . You make the clouds your chariot; / you travel on the wings of the wind. / You make the winds your messenger; / flaming fire, your messengers. . . . [B]y your labor the earth abounds."

Surely, then, she had a sense of God's power at work in our world. And she must certainly have imagined God's presence and power moving among us—like a wind, like a flaming fire—effecting change, causing progress, providing human security.

So Mary could accept in peace and a deep-down joy the fact that the action of the Holy Spirit had caused new life to begin in her and this new life was the word of God now made flesh within her. Mystery? Yes, of course. A mystery to be accepted? Yes indeed. An acceptance made possible by faith? Only by faith. "Be it done unto me according to thy word," said Mary; I'll take it on your word. I believe.

"Through the power of the Holy Spirit," Mary was able not only to conceive but also to believe. Who can say what you are empowered to be and to do by the power of the Holy Spirit? In a certain sense, the Holy Spirit wants to work in and through you to bring Christ forth in your time, in your world. The Spirit wants to work through you but you have to say yes, as Mary did. You have to be willing to bring Christ to life in your own sphere of influence, in your own time here on earth.

So, consider on this Vigil of Christmas in this calendar year—thousands of years after Christ was born in Bethlehem—consider how now, in this calendar year, your yes to the Spirit can make Christ more fully present in a world so deeply in need of redemption. And with the eye of faith, see for a moment tonight how much good might be done "through the power of the Holy Spirit" if only you and other Christians open yourselves, as Mary did, to the will of the Father and the work of the Holy Spirit.

We simply don't believe as firmly and fully as we should. Let your experience here in Word and Sacrament on this Christmas Vigil serve to firm up and deepen your faith so that a literal renewal of the face of the earth may begin right here tonight "through the power of the Holy Spirit."

6

Christmas Mass during the Night

Isaiah 9:1–6; Psalm 96; Titus 2:11–14; Luke 2:1–14

ENTITLEMENT AND INGRATITUDE

Every year, the weeks between Thanksgiving and Christmas provide me with a context for reflection on the relationship between entitlement and ingratitude. Ingratitude can destroy the celebration of Christmas, while gratitude is—or should be—the dominant characteristic of our Christmas celebration.

Thanksgiving, of course, puts the accent where it should be—on giving, saying, and doing thanks. Men and women of faith target God first and foremost for expressions of gratitude when they celebrate the secular feast that we call Thanksgiving Day. Even nonbelievers, I suspect, welcome this American invention of a secular feast day for the occasion it provides to look left and right, if not up to heaven, to say thanks for benefits, if not blessings; and for good luck, if not the generosity of the good Lord. But we are believers—men, women, boys, and girls of faith. We know where to look when we want to give thanks!

Once in the thanks-saying, thanks-giving, thanks-doing mood of late November, it is quite literally a short step to where we are tonight, to Christmas, which, one might expect, should be a season of great gratitude. However, I've noticed at Christmas time as well as in other seasons of the year, a rising sense of entitlement in America, especially among the young. And I've begun to conclude that ingratitude is the infrastructure of entitlement. Think about that—ingratitude is the infrastructure of entitlement, our cultural condition of thinking we deserve everything we have. Entitlement prompts us to make demands, not give thanks.

Ignatius of Loyola once remarked that "ingratitude is at the root of all sinfulness." He was on to something. When ingratitude takes over one's outlook, there is an erosion of a sense of obligation, including moral obligation. "Much obliged" is a way the old American vernacular had of saying thanks. If you have nothing to be thankful for—that is, if you consider yourself to be entitled to everything you have and might receive—you are unencumbered by a sense of any obligation. You are free to be your selfish, solipsistic, narcissistic self. Sadly, we notice a lot of selfishness and narcissism surrounding us at Christmastime.

Total *self-absorption* is another word for sin. And remember, St. Ignatius of Loyola saw ingratitude at the root of all sinfulness, of all self-absorption.

A decade or more ago, I found myself describing students I was then meeting in the college classroom as characterized by a sense of entitlement. They "deserved" good grades, good health, good jobs, and the best of everything the world had to offer. Cultural reinforcement for this attitude of entitlement came, and continues to come, through their entertainment and advertising, their words and music, their images and apparel. They have cures for all their ills, protections from all dangers, solutions for all their problems, answers (with or without the help of a search engine) to all their questions. It is all within reach. It is theirs for the taking. No need to say please. No need to say thanks.

This outlook has seeped down into high school and middle school minds—to the teens and tweens who never say thanks. Good for you if this is not typical of the way things are for you who are gathered here. The absence of a culture of entitlement among you, if that is indeed the case, suggests the presence of a faith-based culture of gratitude.

Still, we will hear ourselves asking over the next few days, what did you get for Christmas? And if you are at all reflective in this season of giving and receiving, you might want to ask yourself—OK—now that you've got it, are you happier than before? Are you disappointed that it isn't what you really wanted or, worse, that it is not as good as something someone you know has received? If any of that sounds familiar to you, if any of that enters into your consciousness in the next few days, beware of the approach of ingratitude and the grip of entitlement.

Many years ago, I pressed a child for a working definition of the word *gift*. "A gift is when somebody gives you something," she said. And I responded: "What if I had borrowed a dollar from you last week and now I'm giving it back. Here, take this dollar. Is that a gift? It fits your definition; you told me that 'a gift is when somebody gives you something' and, here, I'm giving you a dollar." A moment's pondering prompted the youngster to revise her definition and say, "A gift is when you get something you don't deserve."

How true. How very appropriate for Christmas reflection. What a positive indicator that we have, through an awareness of gratitude, a way of protecting ourselves from the virus of entitlement. Christmas will be a good deal merrier and happier for all if we realize that the gifts we exchange are not only undeserved, but that they are symbols to remind us that Christmas is a worldwide celebration of the gift of salvation to which none of us has a claim, except through our faith in Christ Jesus the Lord.

Christ has come. We are freed. All we can be is grateful. And because Christ has come and traced out for us, by his own words and by the example of his life, what we should value and how we should live, we can give a contemporary Christian meaning to the compelling command given so many centuries ago by the Lord through the prophet Micah: "What is good has been explained to you, O man [O woman]; this is what the Lord asks of you: only this, to act justly, to love tenderly, and to walk humbly with your God" (Mic 6:8).

So let's make ours a thoroughly Christian Christmas by acting justly in all our relationships; by loving tenderly our family members and friends and all those whom God puts within reach of our helping hands; and by walking humbly, not arrogantly, but humbly and grate-fully with our God—Emmanuel, who is God with us in Christ Jesus our Lord.

7

Christmas Mass at Dawn

Isaiah 62:11–12; Psalm 97; Titus 3:4–7; Luke 2:15–20

A LIGHT WILL SHINE ON US THIS DAY

The Responsorial Psalm in this Mass at Dawn on Christmas Day is taken from Psalm 97: "A light will shine on us this day: the Lord is born for us."

A light will shine on you today; the Lord is born for you today—on you, for you. You heard other words from Scripture this morning, of course, as you do in every liturgy. For instance, today you heard words from the Prophet Isaiah and from Paul's letter to Titus; and you also heard the familiar Christmas story as recounted for you in the Gospel of Luke. But I want to invite you on this Christmas morning to focus on that one line from Psalm 97. Let those words seep into your soul. Mull them over. Pray over them. Do what Mary is reported in Luke's Gospel account as having done typically and habitually; Luke says that "Mary treasured all these things and reflected on them in her heart."

Treasure these words. "A light will shine on us this day: the Lord is born for us." Savor those words. Ponder them. Personalize them. Let them sink into your heart and pray today that the Holy Spirit will plant there an awareness that you need never again walk in darkness, that you are never alone, that—wonder of wonders—the Lord God is born for you today. For you. For others, yes, of course; indeed for the entire world. But for you as well. Let that awareness sink into your soul.

Don't let yourself be distracted by the Christmas glitter. Don't think today just of good gifts and good food, of family and friends—as important as those considerations are. Don't be lost in the charm of Christmas carols and Christmas trees. Don't focus only on the warm and wonderful Christmas joy that surrounds you—all good, of course;

all to be appreciated and enjoyed. But focus for a moment on yourself and on God's love for you, on God's light and love within you.

Take a moment now to think of those long lapses in your life when you may have lost awareness that the light and love of Christ are around you and within you. Take a moment to recall that you once were lost and now are found. Take some quiet time today to think of Jesus as your light as well as your redeemer.

Sad to say, on any Christmas Day you can look around and see suffering and death, violence and decay, fear and anxiety, hatred and injury. You can see broken promises and smashed hopes. There is reason enough to feel gloomy on Christmas Day or any other day of the year.

But you also see around you goodness and love, generosity and trust, service and life, hope and faith. You see covenants kept and you see fidelity in all its forms at work to keep the human community on course. Modern men and women have cause to claim a peace that is not complacent, a joy that is not naïve. To the extent that this is explainable, the explanation lies in the power of Christmas.

God's power has changed us. God's gift to us in Christ—the light that shines on us today, the Lord who is born for us today—has changed us. The human race once walked in darkness; we now have access to the light.

Outside in our neighborhoods there are Christmas lights on trees and roofs, and in the windows of our homes; they communicate a warmth and welcome to the beholder. But the Christmas light in the face of the believer—in your face—says so much more. It repeats the message of Paul to Titus: "For the grace of God has appeared, saving all and training us to reject godless ways and worldly desires and to live temperately, justly, and devoutly in this age" (Titus 2:11–12).

This message is *readable* for anyone who picks up the New Testament. It is *audible* wherever the good news is proclaimed. And it is intended to be *visible* in the life of the believer. This is the power of Christmas. This is the light in our world today.

8

Christmas Mass during the Day

Isaiah 52:7–10; Psalm 98; Hebrews 1:1–6; John 1:1–18

"ALL THE ENDS OF THE EARTH WILL BEHOLD THE SALVATION OF OUR GOD"

The words of Isaiah that you heard in today's first reading encourage you to see the big picture, to take the broad view. "All the ends of the earth will behold the salvation of our God." Make that perspective your own on this Christmas Day. Rise above it all; pull back, if you will, and savor the sight of salvation stretching over all the ends of the earth. That's what happened on the first Christmas Day.

For many years, I have turned on Christmas Day to words written by Karl Stern. He was a psychiatrist, a convert from Judaism to Catholicism, who expressed in a single paragraph in his 1951 autobiography, *The Pillar of Fire*, feelings from a searching human heart and put them in words that catch the dimensions of wonder that Isaiah had in mind in referring to "all the ends of the earth." Listen to Karl Stern:

> I used to sit on a bench on Primrose Hill and look over all the City of London. If it were true, I used to think, that God had become man, and that his life and death had a personal meaning to every single person among all those millions of existences spent in the stench of slums, in a horizonless world, in the suffocating anguish of enmities, sickness and dying—if that were true, it would be something tremendously worth living for. To think that Someone knocked on all those millions of dark doors, beckoning and promising to each in an altogether unique way. Christ challenged not only the apparent chaos of history but the meaninglessness of personal existence.

I have no idea where Primrose Hill is, but I know that each of us has a real or imaginary "perch" from which we can look out over any city or any part of the world. Locate yourself there for a moment now.

Someone did indeed knock on all those dark doors across the earth. Someone did reach out to every single person in millions of existences throughout history. And that someone was and is Jesus Christ whose birth we celebrate today. It is in, for, and with that special someone that you, along with Karl Stern, can say you find life tremendously worth living. Why? Because his coming changed everything. We now have purpose. We have meaning in our lives.

Christmas marked the "fullness of time." God stepped into human history in a decisive, declarative, salvific way to work the redemption of the human race. God made something special happen.

If we believe in the Lordship of Christ and if we believe that the Father raised him from the dead, we too shall move through death to life, as he did. The Word moved from the everlasting to the transitory and back to the everlasting, and showed us the way. Let me take you to the Letter to the Colossians to assist you in making the contemplative stretch that I'm urging you to consider today:

He is the image of the invisible God,
the firstborn of all creation.
For in him were created all things
in heaven and on earth,
the visible and the invisible,
whether thrones or dominions
or principalities or powers;
all things were created through him
and for him.
He is before all things,
and in him all things hold together.
He is the head of the body, the church.
He is the beginning,
the firstborn from the dead,
that in all things he might be preeminent.
For in him

all the fullness was pleased to dwell,
and through him
to reconcile all things for him,
making peace by the blood of his cross. . . .
(Col 1:15–20)

Mention of the cross at the very end of that reflection suggests to me, and I make the suggestion now to you, that there is a link between what we celebrate on Christmas and what we contemplate on Calvary. In fact, I recall receiving a Christmas card one year that had a stark representation of the wood of the cross beside a sketch of the wooden manger, and the artwork was accompanied by these words of Jesus to Pilate: "For this was I born, for this I came into the world" (John 18:37). There you have it: the wood of the manger and the wood of the cross— linked inextricably in the life, words, and deeds of Jesus Christ, linked as well in the life of every follower of Christ.

Now I recognize that all this is a bit heavy for Christmas Day. I don't intend it to be. I don't at all want to distract you from the family love, the warmth, and joy that should have a place in your hearts today. But neither do I want all that high-hearted joy to distract you from the profound theological truth that the wood of the manger and the wood of the cross should be linked in your consciousness and resident in your life.

It is all so special, so sacred, so worthy of reflection, so congenial to adoration. Savor it; ponder it. Let it touch your soul today and from the depth of your soul thus touched, hear yourself say, "All the ends of the earth will behold the salvation of our God."

9

Feast of the Holy Family, Sunday in the Octave of Christmas

Sirach 3:2–7, 12–14; Psalm 128; Colossians 3:12–21; Luke 2:22–40

FAMILY FIRST

This is Holy Family Sunday. The focus is on Jesus, Mary, and Joseph—the original Holy Family—but our thoughts must also turn today to the idea of family, the importance of family, and the future of family here in the United States of America.

The Gospel story you just heard from Luke puts you in the company of Mary and Joseph, along with their infant son Jesus, whom they were taking into the temple in Jerusalem because they were following what is written in the Law, namely, that "Every first-born male shall be consecrated to the Lord." This is what is sometimes referred to as the Presentation of the Child Jesus in the Temple. It is familiar to you as one of the joyful mysteries of the Rosary.

It is a scene that many of you parents have made your own by carrying a newborn son or daughter into church, in some cases even placing him or her on the altar, but in all instances presenting your child to God and asking God's blessing and protection on your newborn child. The child is God's gift to you; the presentation of that child in church is your gift to God. The gesture invites God's blessing on you and helps to constitute you—parents and child—as a holy family. Repeated with the birth of each new child, you grow as a holy family.

If you haven't done that with a newborn child, you should.

As you well know, the idea of family is under attack in our country and elsewhere in the world today. Your own immediate, domestic, holy family is an important unit in the line of defense of family that is needed today. The idea of family, of course, is grounded in the chaste love of a man for a woman and a woman for a man, ushering in new life that depends not just on food to eat and air to breathe, but on love—the love of a father and a mother—to survive. Love is the atmosphere, the environment, of family life. There may be poverty in the picture, as there was in the original Holy Family of Jesus, Mary, and Joseph, but love can overcome poverty. There may be danger in the picture, as there was when Herod threatened to kill the holy child and Joseph and Mary fled with their child to Egypt—another instance of love overcoming fear. Without love, the family falters; with love, the family grows stronger by the day.

Luke's Gospel story introduces you to the elderly Simeon and to the widow Anna, "who was constantly in the temple," and you heard their words of praise of this holy child. You also know that Joseph, the father in the original Holy Family, was a "just" man and that Mary, his wife, was uniquely favored by the Lord. But even they had to meet the responsibilities of parenthood day by day, one day at a time, one year after another, after they "returned to Galilee and their own town of Nazareth" where "[t]he child grew in size and strength, filled with wisdom, and the grace of God was upon him."

We honor them today—the Holy Family. But we will do well also today to give some prayerful thought to the importance of family and the future of family here in the United States. The family needs some shoring up; it needs imaginative care and all the prayerful support we can provide.

Those of you who are parents know that there is no escaping the responsibility, no walking away from the twenty-four-hours-a-day, seven-days-a-week relationship you have with your spouse and with your offspring. Yes, of course, there are some who desert, defect, disengage themselves from family ties, but that is not an option for you. Without your family love, your community will be less fully human. Without your family life, your nation will be weaker. Family is reinforcement for our fragility. None of us is perfect, but our imperfection is overcome by love, by family love.

Now you might fairly look at me and ask what do I, an unmarried celibate, know about all this. And you have a point. As I've often remarked to students, I live in that home for unwed fathers that is called the Jesuit community at whatever university I happen to be assigned to. But I've been a beneficiary of family life; I'll always be grateful for that. And I'm an observer of what works and what doesn't in contemporary family living. So I'm here to cheer you on today, to encourage you to be faithful to your marriage vows and to live up to the demands of family life.

Let me give you a list of elements of family life that are worthy of your consideration today. Not all of these together at any one moment, but a proper mix of each in appropriate portions at the right time, is a good recipe for successful family living: (1) prayer (you are at prayer right now; you'll have opportunities for prayer at home before meals, before retiring); (2) food (you'll be sharing food together soon at your own family table and you should try to do that on a daily basis; you can also share in the shopping, preparation, and cleanup associated with the use of food in your family); (3) books, magazines, and newspapers (reading aloud at home, reading to each other, reading for fun); (4) homework; (5) household chores; (6) music (lessons, practice, live, recorded; "the house without a piano is a home without a soul"); (7) sports (in the neighborhood, at school, your favorite teams); (8) family watching television together; (9) trips; (10) vacations. There will also be weddings and baptisms, first communions and graduations, illness and funerals, shared family projects. All these elements and so much more constitute family life.

The new technologies are part of family life today. Regrettably, some of them are isolating and privatizing and destructive of family unity, and they have to be controlled.

Creative family living means participating sometimes, but not always; it means specializing in some very few activities (being really good at something), choosing what not to do, and never forcing others to do what they don't want to do. But creative family living requires parents to be mindful of their responsibility to provide the wherewithal for this kind of activity. It can weave the fabric of family. It provides the memories that testify to rich family experiences.

So talk to one another today, all you family members. Give yourselves a checkup on the quality of your family life. Family doesn't just happen; you've got to make it happen. And there is no possibility of a holy family unless there is a genuine loving family in place providing a foundation for growth in holiness. Let's pray for one another today as our shared effort to strengthen family life continues.

10

January 1, Octave of Christmas, Solemnity of Mary, Mother of God

Numbers 6:22–27; Psalm 67; Galatians 4:4–7; Luke 2:16–21

"THE SHEPHERDS WENT IN HASTE TO BETHLEHEM"

The Church honors Mary in a special way today; it is the Solemnity of Mary, Mother of God. That title says it all—Mother of God.

How can God, creator of all, who existed before the world or anyone or anything in the world existed, how can God be said to have a mother? Only because of the scene laid out for you today in the Gospel of Luke—the scene that caused the shepherds to go "in haste to Bethlehem." This is the scene that you can hold for a few moments now in your imagination. In that scene you see a young mother—Mary; and you see her infant son—Jesus.

You know, by faith, which is to say you believe, that Jesus is divine. Jesus is the second person of the Blessed Trinity. You believe that yours is one God in three divine persons, a God who has no beginning and no end. And you celebrate in this Christmas season the birth of the second person—present from all eternity as the Divine Word—but born in time as Jesus Christ. The Divine Word has taken human flesh in the womb of Mary and is born to us as Christ—as the Messiah, the anointed one.

There could have been no Christmas without a mother; and here she is—Mary, the Mother of God. Think about that—without a mother, there is no Christmas.

Like the shepherds, we now rush over to Bethlehem to see it all. We are caught up in wonder. We are indescribably grateful. Why? Because, as the selection in today's liturgy from the Letter to the Galatians puts it, "When the designated time had come, God sent forth his Son born of a woman." And that woman, as you know, was Mary. She is, therefore, the Mother of God. We rush over in this exercise of the imagination to see her, to thank her, and to adore her son.

Wonder of wonders, his mother is also our mother. Mary is mother to each one of us. And how do we know that? Well, Jesus, you will remember, hanging on the cross, looked into the face of Mary who was standing there and he told her to look at John, his beloved disciple who was also standing there; and Jesus said to her, "behold your son" (John 19:26). "Then he said to the disciple [John, a stand-in for all of us], 'behold, your mother.'" And the beloved disciple, Scripture says, "took her into his home."

You too should take her now into the home of your heart. She is your mother. She has held you in her heart all these years, and continues to do so. But today the Church is asking you to become more fully conscious of the fact that your mother Mary is indeed the Mother of God.

There she is in poverty and simplicity—on the ground—in Bethlehem; and here she is in glory and honor—in heaven now—as Mother of God. And just as she responded to the human needs of her newborn son there in Bethlehem, she is at the ready now to respond to your needs because she is your mother too.

It is a beautiful moment in so many Catholic funerals, when, after communion, the "Ave Maria" is sung. It is as if the deceased person wanted to express public appreciation to Mary for her motherly care. She is acknowledged in that lovely hymn as "sancta Maria, Mater Dei"—holy Mary, Mother of God. And so she is, and has been, and will remain forever. You may want to make a note today, to be left with your final effects, that you want the "Ave Maria" to be sung in your funeral liturgy because of your love for Mary and the debt you owe to the Mother of God.

The imaginary visit you have made today along with the shepherds "over to Bethlehem" has taken you to the side of Mary. She welcomes you there, wants you there; you belong to her and she belongs to you.

Never make the mistake of thinking that you are alone on your journey of faith in this world. You have a mother's guidance, a mother's care. She is a patient, caring presence in your life. She knows that you might disappoint her at times, but she will never forget you, never let you down. *Sancta Maria, Mater Dei, ora pro nobis—peccatoribus—nunc et in hora mortis nostrae. Amen.*

Admittedly, we are all sinners (*peccatoribus*). Happily she is with us now and will be there with us and for us at the hour of death (*nunc et in hora mortis nostrae. Amen.*).

Honor her by thanking her today on this the Solemnity of Mary, Mother of God.

11

Second Sunday after Christmas

Sirach 24:1–4, 8–12; Psalm 147; Ephesians 1:3–6, 15–18; John 1:1–18

"GOD CHOSE US IN HIM [CHRIST JESUS] BEFORE THE WORLD BEGAN"

These Christmas season readings offer what I like to think of as "ponderables"—profound realities for our prayerful consideration. Permit me to help you enter into these ponderables for a few reflective moments today.

In the first reading, the selection you heard from the Book of Sirach (one of the so-called wisdom books in the Old Testament), you heard these words: "Before all ages, in the beginning, he [the Most High] created me, and through all ages I shall not cease to be." Let that thought play out in your spatial imagination. Try to compute the dimensions of that thought in relationship to yourself. "Before all ages, in the beginning, he created me, and through all ages I shall not cease to be."

And from the selection you heard in the second reading from St. Paul's Letter to the Ephesians you will recall these words: "God chose us in him [Christ] before the world began to be holy and blameless in his sight, to be full of love." St. Paul surely saw himself from that perspective and that's the perspective I'm hoping you will take for a few moments now. In addition to the words I just quoted from the Letter to the Ephesians, listen to these words from Paul's Letter to the Galatians (1:15): "[F]rom my mother's womb God set me apart and called me through his grace." Paul clearly had an awareness of that perspective of connectedness with God, in Christ, from the very beginning. Paul carried that awareness with him. That's the perspective I'm inviting you to take right now.

And today's Gospel reading, the opening words of the Fourth Gospel, are striking: "Through him [the Word] all things came into being." Realize that this includes you and me; we came into being through the creating word of God.

All these references, you will notice, locate you in the mind of God from the very beginning of creation. You were there, with God, from the beginning. So try to let your mind stretch for a few moments now to take all this in. As you do, you will be undertaking a mental construction of the framework you need to have a balanced perspective on your life and place in this world—on your way, as you are, to eternity, to eternal life with the God who has known you, chosen you, and loved you from the beginning.

Sad, isn't it, that we so easily lose this perspective, sad that we lose consciousness of our connectedness with the love that God had and has for us from the beginning? Obviously, you can't be thinking about this all the time, but you can carry this awareness with you at an unconscious level, just below the surface of consciousness. That's why reflecting on these ponderables as Christmas recedes into the past is a good idea. Such reflection will file these truths away for easy retrieval in the future, for moments when you need to be reminded that you are not alone, that you are not forgotten, that you do indeed have purpose here, and that you carry with you wherever you go the promise of eternal life.

So repeat with reverence and gratitude these words now: "God chose us in him [Christ] before the world began." "In the beginning, he [the Most High] created me and through all the ages I shall not cease to be." And after you return home today, pick up your New Testament and turn to the opening words of the Fourth Gospel; you heard them proclaimed as the Gospel reading in this Mass today. It would not be difficult to make the case that the saddest line in all the literature of the world is this one verse in that Prologue to the Gospel of St. John: "He was in the world, and the world came to be through him, but the world did not know him."

The Prologue refers to him, as "the Word"—"In the beginning was the Word, and the Word was with God, and the Word was God." He, God, came into a world full of persons who owed their very existence to him, and yet they did not recognize him for what and for who he was.

And the very next verse drives the point home, to his very own people: "He came to what was his own, but his own people did not accept him." Those words underscore the tragedy of lost opportunity for those who neither recognized their Creator nor welcomed their Savior when he stepped into their history, and not their history only, but into their human nature and human flesh.

I'm offering you now a second chance, so to speak, an opportunity to recognize him, to welcome him, to thank him, to love him of course, and to carry him in your heart as you move away from Christmas back toward Ordinary Time.

12

Epiphany

Isaiah 60:1–6; Psalm 72; Ephesians 3:2–3, 5–6; Matthew 2:1–12

LITTLE CHRISTMAS

Many years ago, they used to call it "Little Christmas," the Feast of the Epiphany. It occurred on January 6th and only then were representations of the three wise men, bearing gifts of gold, frankincense, and myrrh, added to the Christmas crib in churches and homes. The wise men that you meet today in Matthew's Gospel came from "the east," from distant lands, into the full glare of this revelation of God made man.

I've always liked the name "Epiphany." It comes from the Greek prefix *epi*, which means "bump up against," and the Greek verb *phainein*, which means "shine forth." I like to think of Epiphany as not only the appearance of the newborn Christ—Christ the King—to the nations (the *gentes* or, as we say, gentiles) represented by the three wise men, but as the breaking of the newborn Messiah, the Christ of Christmas, into the broader world's awareness. He was born, as you know, a Jew in Bethlehem of Judea. But here he is on a broader stage—bumping up against, breaking into the awareness of the whole world through the agency of these three figures known to us as the "Magi."

The brief second reading from the Letter to the Ephesians underscores the significance of it all: "in Christ Jesus the Gentiles are now co-heirs with the Jews. Members of the same body and sharers of the promise through the preaching of the gospel."

But you have to ask yourself now these many years later as we are well into the twenty-first century of the Christian era, what about those who seem not yet to have heard the preaching of the gospel? How about those who seem not yet to be sharing in "the promise"? What about the enormous portion of the world's population that is not Christian? We might properly say, "not yet" Christian, because we believe that Jesus came to all, to the entire human race, to men and women of North and South, East, and West, to all the ends of the earth. It is clear that much shining forth and breaking through remains to be done. It should also be clear that this shining forth and breaking through remains to be done by us who call ourselves Christians.

Epiphany reminds us that we are expected to be attractive. That's right, attractive. Those around us, whether near or far, should see in us something that attracts them to the truths that we hold dear and to which we bear witness with our lives. There are language differences, of course, and there are cultural differences; there is geographic diversity. And yet "in Christ Jesus," we—all of us—are meant to be "members of the same body and sharers of the promise through the preaching of the gospel."

What about that preaching? We are called, we Christians, to be like Christ. We are called to be men and women of the Beatitudes. We are called to love one another, not simply as we love ourselves, but as Christ has loved us—to the point of laying down our lives for one another at home, at work, at every stage, and in every circumstance of our lives here on earth. That's what it means to be a Christian. That's what we should be showing forth for all the world to see. Some of us are called to talk about it, to explain it. All of us are called to live it, to proclaim it not necessarily by spoken word but by the example of our lives. It is a sobering thought as we celebrate Epiphany to consider how we might not be holding up our side of the bargain, how we might be failing to show forth for the world to see what we really believe.

Listen again to the words from the Prophet Isaiah that opened the first reading in this Epiphany liturgy and apply those words to yourself: "Rise up in splendor, Jerusalem! Your light has come, the glory of God shines upon you. See darkness covers the earth, and thick clouds cover the peoples; but upon you the Lord shines, and over you appears his glory. Nations shall walk by your light, and kings by your shining radiance. Raise your eyes and look about; they all gather and come to you. . . ."

That's the message of Epiphany—"your light has come . . . upon you the Lord shines." Take that message to heart today and ask yourself, "Does anyone notice? Do I show forth anything that reflects the presence of Christ in our world, anything that suggests the wisdom of his words and the practical value of his way of life?" "If I'm not giving witness to that, can I really call myself Christian?"

The question before us today my friends is, "What does it mean to be an Epiphany Christian?" And the answer to that question can only emerge from the depths of your Christian heart.

13

Baptism of the Lord

Isaiah 42:1–4, 6–7; Psalm 29; Acts 10:34–38; Matthew 1:7–11

THE THEME OF JOHN'S PREACHING

The Gospel reading that you just heard from St. Matthew tells you that "the theme of John's preaching was: 'One more powerful than I is to come after me. I am not fit to stoop and untie his sandal straps.'"

This is a reference to John the Baptist, who is not to be confused with John the beloved disciple, the youngest apostle. John the Baptist is the one who spent time in the desert; he is a rugged, independent person, a cousin of Jesus. His mission in this world was to "prepare the way of the Lord."

John the Baptist is usually not on anyone's list of favorite saints. He is not the gentle Francis of Assisi, or the faithful and ever-reliable St. Joseph. He is the advance man, the self-effacing one who made sure he was not mistaken for Jesus. "I am not fit to stoop and untie his sandal straps," said John with reference to Jesus and John's special role in readying the path on which Jesus would walk.

John embodies a virtue that I like to call "humbition." That word is an amalgam of two words—humility ("I'm not worthy to untie his sandal straps") and ambition (John did not shrink from the great challenge of preparing the way of the Lord). John was, in the best sense of the word, humbitious.

Each of us should consider today, as we contemplate the baptism of the Lord, how we might, these many centuries later, participate in the ministry of John the Baptist. He was the advance man. He prepared the way of the Lord. He cleared the path. He, speaking of himself, once said, "I must decrease; he (Jesus) must increase." That was the pattern of John's mission; that was his task.

Much needs to be done in our own day to prepare the way of the Lord. That preparation has to happen within the hearts of men and women to whom the Lord wants to come, but is impeded from coming by human pride, human self-centeredness resident there in the human heart. You who are Christian, you who have already welcomed the Christ into your heart, you can now be like John the Baptist and work by word and example, as John did, to prepare the way of the Lord. Today this might mean helping others to lower the barriers within them—within their minds and hearts—to acceptance of a countercultural Christ who wants to break into their consciousness, who wants to possess their souls, who wants to be their Savior, their model. This does not mean arguing with them; it simply means permitting the quiet persuasion of your good example to become more visible.

Somehow or other those who do not yet know Christ must first see him in you. People who saw John the Baptist wondered aloud whether he might be the promised messiah; something they saw in him prompted this speculation. What might others see in you that will turn their thoughts to higher realms, to the goodness that is embodied in the person of Christ?

There was self-effacement that was visible in the person of John the Baptist. There was a concern for others. He displayed energy and zeal as well as prayer and fasting. But remember, he was also humbitious!

Dress John the Baptist in contemporary garb and imagine him to be walking not in the desert but on our city streets. How might he stand out today? What might set him apart? And how might these differences serve to attract others to, rather than repel them from, the message of John that needs to be repeated today, namely, that the Messiah is in our midst, knocking at our doors, awaiting our response?

Recall that the theme of John's preaching was: "One more powerful than I is to come after me." How do you communicate to others by your words, your example, your lifestyle, that one far more powerful that any of us has indeed come to save all of us, is indeed here among us, is available to meet our needs right now?

It is just possible that religion, as we practice it, gets in the way of this witness. I say that not to upset you but only to alert you to the fact that religious observance by the most observant can be off-putting to others who are still seeking and searching. It seems to me that the community that was drawn to John the Baptist—the community that was there on the banks of the Jordan River when Jesus came forward to be baptized—was an open, accepting community.

How open and accepting are you? How open and accepting is your community of faith? To what extent are smiles the sign of your presence to one another, and of your collective presence to those who feel drawn to you? Too many unsmiling Christians go their separate ways displaying faces like fists instead of opening their eyes, hearts, minds, and church doors to unknown others who are searching for meaning and hungering for the love that is available to them in the person of Jesus Christ—"the one more powerful than I" whom John the Baptist served and who now depends on you!

III
Lent

. . . .

14

First Sunday of Lent

Genesis 9:8–15; Psalm 25; 1 Peter 3:18–22; Mark 1:12–15

COVENANT AND KINGDOM

There are two words I'll ask you to wrap your hearts and minds around this morning and those two words are *covenant* and *kingdom*.

Covenant was mentioned five times in that relatively brief selection from the Book of Genesis that you heard as the first reading in today's Mass. Five times. God said to Noah: (1) "See I am now establishing my covenant with you…;" (2) "I will establish my covenant with you, that never again shall all bodily creatures be destroyed by the waters of a flood;" (3) "This is the sign that I am giving for all ages to come, of the covenant between me and you…;" (4) "I set my bow [my rainbow] in the clouds to serve as a sign of the covenant between me and the earth;" and (5) "I will recall the covenant I have made between me and you.…"

What is a covenant? If you consult your dictionary, you will see that a covenant is a formal binding agreement, a compact. It is a promise that is locked in, and locked up permanently. When God spoke to Moses and through Moses to "all ages to come," an irrevocable commitment was made, an unconditional promise that God will not destroy the earth. We can count on that, although we have no assurance, no promise, that God will prevent us from destroying ourselves! That is one reason why we are so serious about praying for peace—permanent peace—in a nuclear age like ours when we hold in our hands destructive power that is beyond all imagining.

Now *covenant* is used in other contexts too. We speak of the marriage covenant—that unconditional promise, that firm irrevocable commitment that constitutes a marriage, a commitment that binds a man and woman in a relationship of love that lasts until death. And, as you know, the sacramental marriage covenant is sealed with God's saving grace.

We speak of covenants between nations and between contracting parties. Admittedly, these are not sacred covenants, but they are serious commitments.

God made other covenants that we read about in the Bible. One with Abraham, another with Moses. And in both cases the commitment is permanent. To Abraham, for example, God said: "…I am making you the father of a host of nations.…I will maintain my covenant with you and your descendants after you throughout the ages as an everlasting pact, to be your God and the God of your descendants after you" (Gen 17:5–7). And to Moses God said: "I will look with favor upon you, and make you fruitful and numerous, as I carry out my covenant with you.…I will set my Dwelling among you, and will not disdain you. Ever present in your midst, I will be your God, and you will be my people" (Lev 26:9, 11–12). And in each case, God acknowledged that those with whom he made his covenant were free to break away, but if they chose to break the covenant, there would be sad consequences.

That is why I invite you to connect the notion of *covenant* with *kingdom* this morning. Jesus, as you met him moments ago stepping into his public life in the opening chapter of Mark's Gospel, declares: "This is the time of fulfillment. The kingdom of God is at hand. Repent, and believe in the gospel."

Let's take that three-sentence declaration as a three-part connection between covenant and kingdom. We, dear friends, are a people of God, a Church, on our way to a kingdom. We're not yet there. We pray, whenever we say the Lord's Prayer, and take careful note of the words, "Thy kingdom come." It is not yet here, it is on its way; or, to put that in other words, we are on our way toward the kingdom.

Why is it that now—twenty centuries after Jesus declared the kingdom of God to be "at hand"—why is it that the kingdom has not yet come? Jesus tells you why. He added to his proclamation of the kingdom being at hand, this instruction, this preparatory condition: "Repent, and believe in the gospel." We need to repent. We need not only to repent of sin, we need an attitudinal turnaround, a change of heart, a value reversal. We have to allow ourselves to think and live in harmony with Gospel values. Not as this world thinks and values, but as the Gospel Jesus proclaimed and died for invites us to think and value.

The kingdom of God is not a place; it is a rule or reign. It is the rule of God's law and love over human hearts. It is a reign of justice, love, and peace. Why has the kingdom not yet come? Because we, in our stubborn sinfulness, refuse to lower the barriers in our lives to the coming kingdom. We prefer hatred to love, injustice to justice, war to peace. And hatred, injustice, and war are all barriers to the coming kingdom.

"This is the time of fulfillment," Jesus said, and that amounted to saying that the covenant that God made for us and with us, through Noah, Abraham, and Moses, is ready for full realization. If we refuse to let love, justice, and peace bloom and grow, if we resist, or worse, repudiate the covenant's requirements of love, justice, and peace in human affairs, we postpone the time of fulfillment; we keep the kingdom "at hand," but at arm's length.

Covenant and *kingdom*. Connect them in your thoughts and prayers today. Connect them to your Lenten observance. "Repent, and believe in the Gospel," Jesus said. Those words, or words close to them, were said when the ashes were put on your forehead last Wednesday.

The Gospel in which you believe lays out the rules of life for you, the styles and ways of life that are patterned after the style and life of Christ. Lent provides you with another opportunity for a midcourse correction. Where are your areas of infidelity? Where are the fault lines on your side of the covenant God has made with you? Where are your commitments in need of repair? That's where the Lenten project begins for you this year.

And to keep it all close to home, down to earth and practical, look to the covenants you have made that affect your daily life, look to your marriage covenant, your family commitments, your contracts and promises, attend to all of them as part of your Lenten observance. Consider what might be done to shore up your part of those covenants and then determine to go ahead and do it as part of your Lenten observance this year.

15

Second Sunday of Lent

Genesis 22:1–2, 9a, 10–13, 15–18; Psalm 116; Romans 8:31b–34;
Mark 9:2–10

ON BEING "PUT TO THE TEST"

Let me organize this homily around three points, each taken from a
verse in each of the three readings proclaimed in today's Liturgy of the
Word. First, the opening sentence from the first reading, the selection
from the Book of Genesis: "God put Abraham to the test." Second, the
famous Christian rallying cry first articulated by St. Paul in his Letter
to the Romans: "If God is for us, who can be against us?" And third,
"he was transfigured before them," writes St. Mark, who then records
the voice of God speaking from the clouds and saying: "This is my
beloved Son. Listen to him."

(1) On being "put to the test," (2) on becoming convinced that "If
God is for us, who can be against us?" and (3) on letting the lesson of
the transfiguration work its magic on us—these are our three points
for consideration in this Lenten liturgy.

The story of Abraham's obedience to what surely seems to us to be
an unfair and completely unreasonable command from God, namely,
that Abraham should sacrifice his son, "offer him up as a holocaust,"
is familiar to us, but it makes us more than a little uncomfortable. If
you go to the fuller text in the Book of Genesis, you'll notice that the
dutiful son Isaac carries the wood for the fire on his own shoulders.
Innocently, he asks where is the sheep that would be needed for the
sacrifice and his father assures him that "God himself will provide the
sheep for the holocaust," as he, Abraham, proceeds to move obediently
forward to the point of drawing his knife on the verge of sacrificing
his own son. "But the Lord's messenger called to him from heaven,

'Abraham, Abraham!' 'Here I am,' he answered. 'Do not lay your hand on the boy,' said the messenger. 'Do not do the least thing to him. I know now how devoted you are to God, since you did not withhold from me your own beloved son.'" And, as the story in Genesis goes on to say, Abraham looked around and saw a ram, which he took and offered as a holocaust in place of his son.

This is a classic case of "being put to the test." We pray daily, do we not, "lead us not into temptation," and that, of course, means "do not put us to the test," at least do not test us beyond out strength. "Why test us at all?" you might ask. That's a fair question. It's been raised in modern times in Rabbi Harold Kushner's famous book title: *When Bad Things Happen to Good People*. He asks, "why?" We all find ourselves at times asking, "why?" "Why me?" "Why this?" "Why now?" And the more we puzzle and ponder over the issue, the closer we should be getting to an appreciation of these tests as turnstiles on our journey of faith.

Trust God. Put your trust in God. Believe with all your heart that God indeed "will provide." Provide? Isn't that what providence means? Why do we apply that word *providence* to banks and insurance companies and neglect to apply it to ourselves? Trust in God's providence for you. Believe that God will indeed provide.

Take a few minutes sometime during Lent to make the Stations of the Cross, to follow the path, as the representations on the walls of churches and chapels invite you, to follow the Way of the Cross, realizing that Jesus traveled that journey for you.

If you turn to the Fourth Gospel, the Gospel of John, to orient yourself for this devotional exercise, you will notice early on in the nineteenth chapter (v. 17), where John describes the crucifixion of Jesus, these words: "So they took Jesus, and carrying the cross himself he went out to what is called the Place of the Skull, in Hebrew, Golgotha." "Carrying the cross himself." Perhaps you will find in that phrase a gentle echo of the Genesis account of Isaac carrying on his own shoulders the wood for his sacrifice. And just as the fatherly love of Abraham was fixed on his son during that anguished journey of faith leading to the mount of sacrifice, so the love of God the Father hovers over Jesus at every step on his Way of the Cross.

"God put Abraham to the test."

God permitted Jesus to be tested.

God will let tests come your way from time to time. And God's love will never fail you in those faith-deepening opportunities, those moments of your own personal participation in the paschal mystery, which is for us, of course, the Christian riddle of moving through defeat to victory, disappointment to satisfaction, failure to success, and, eventually, through death to life.

Convinced of this, move on to point number two and say with St. Paul, "If God is for us, who can be against us?" Say it aloud for a moment now. Say it again, "If God is for us, who can be against us?" Do you believe that? Are you *confident*? *Con-fide* means "with faith." Faith sustains us when we are, as we surely will be from time to time, "put to the test."

Confidence is not arrogance. The man or woman of Christian faith knows, to the extent that any of this is at all knowable, that he or she cannot go it alone. Our faith is in God, not in our own power. Our faith is in a God who is all-powerful and who loves us beyond all imagining.

On then to point number three: the spectacle of a transfigured Jesus and the words heard breaking out from above: "This is my beloved Son. Listen to him." The wise and considerate Jesus knew that the brutal events that were coming when he would be arrested, scourged, and crucified, would shake the faith of his followers beyond all ordinary limits. His followers would surely be put to the test. So he chose to be transfigured briefly in their presence. His clothes became dazzling white. Towering figures from the past, Moses and Elijah, appeared in their midst. Ordinary reality was transformed momentarily into extraordinary dimensions to impress upon the disciples that their leader was special, powerful, capable of transcending limits, and all of this so that they would not lose heart, not lose confidence in him or in themselves, that they would not lose faith.

Let me encourage you, each one of you, to place yourselves with the disciples in the presence of the transfigured Jesus. Let me urge you to be sufficiently confident—faith-filled—not at all arrogant, just *confidently* Christian—to permit yourself to bask in the glory of the transfigured Christ and apply to yourself the reassuring words: This is my beloved son; this is my beloved daughter.

Don't back away or squirm aside from acceptance of the gift God wants you to have, namely, that you are good and graced and gifted, not because you earned God's love, but because God chose to see you and love you in the person of Jesus Christ who gave his life for you.

Some years ago, the Gallup organization published the results of a poll on how Americans link up faith and everyday living. They found a gap between what Americans believe and how they act. About 80 percent of the people polled said they feel connected with God, had an "inner commitment" with God, but only 70 percent of those respondents had anything resembling an "outer commitment," which would mean letting their belief in God spill over into service to others.

Seventy-six percent of Christians agreed that all people, regardless of race, creed, or wealth, are loved by God. But only 44 percent said the notion that "God calls me to be involved in the lives of the poor and suffering" applies to them. One of the researchers commenting on that point, said: "I think what that's telling us is that it's easy to believe something; it's harder to put it into play."

That well may be. Let me simply leave you with the reminder that when the disciples came down the mountain after the transfiguration experience, they settled down, got to work, and put their faith into play. And that's the challenge for all of us disciples who are working our way toward Easter.

16

Third Sunday of Lent

Exodus 20:1–17; Psalm 19; 1 Corinthians 1:22–25; John 2:13–25 [or, Exodus 17:3–7; Psalm 95; Romans 5:1–2, 5–8; John 4:5–42]

WORDS OF EVERLASTING LIFE

"Lord, you have the words of everlasting life." So says Psalm 19 and so we believe, as we pray that psalm to God today. "Lord, you have the words of everlasting life."

"Come, let us sing joyfully to the Lord," Psalm 95 urges; "let us acclaim the rock of our salvation. Let us come into his presence with thanksgiving; let us joyfully sing psalms to him." But what cause do we have to sing joyfully, or, indeed, to be joyful on this the Third Sunday of Lent and the first Sunday of this war of ours in Iraq? [This homily was first delivered in 2003.]

There is little cause for joy. There is good reason for anxiety and fear. We are at war. Lives have already been lost. More lives—American lives; Iraqi lives; lives of men and women in uniform; lives of men, women, and children who do not bear arms—more lives will be lost. And so we pray for peace, for an end to hostilities, for a resolution of the differences that have produced this crisis that has erupted into armed conflict. We approach the Lord and say, "Lord, you have the words of everlasting life." And in this eucharistic celebration of word and sacrament, we hope to hear the word of the Lord. We hope it will strengthen us, comfort us, guide us.

Psalm 95 goes on to have us say: "Come, let us bow down in worship; let us kneel before the Lord who made us. For he is our God, and we are the people he shepherds, the flock he guides."

I'm doubly troubled on this Sunday and, if you think about it, I suspect that you are troubled too. I'm troubled that we are at war, and I'm

58

troubled at the threat of terrorist reprisals. I'm troubled at the destruction of life and property in Iraq; I'm troubled at the thought of sudden terrorist attacks on life and property here at home. I'm troubled by the talk of duct tape and sealed-off refuges, and I'm frightened at the thought of no safe refuge against biological or chemical weapons. Against such, I know I may find myself defenseless.

That's what I mean when I say I'm twice troubled today as I turn my troubled heart to the Lord and say, "Lord, you have the words of everlasting life." And I ask the Lord to speak those words to me today. Do you share my feeling, dear friends? Do you join my prayer?

As men and women of faith, we surely do not want to be coldly fatalistic, saying, so to speak, whatever comes will come. If I die, I die. I cannot escape the fate that is mine. No; none of that for us. Fatalism is unworthy of our faith, which places us, quite literally, above all that. As men and women of faith, we turn to our Lord who does indeed have not only the words of everlasting life, but, who has promised us a share in his own everlasting life. Our Lord has promised us eternal life—possession of everlasting life—the promise that we will live forever. And in that promise, we find strength in the face of discouragement, comfort in the face of anxiety, courage in the face of fear, peace in the face of wartime worry and terrorist threats.

Yes, it could happen that we could die "before our time," as some would say. We could die as casualties of terrorism. We defend ourselves as best we can, knowing all the while that there is no defense against some forms of malice; knowing all the while that our best efforts and most prudent measures may fail to protect us from evil and hateful forces intent on doing us in.

I don't mean to disturb you, or trouble you, in speaking of these realities. I do mean, however, to open your minds to a profound reality of our faith. Let me put it this way. As a priest, I have found myself enquiring from time to time how someone who had serious surgery in the recent past, or who was recovering from a serious accident, is doing now. And I've been amused often to hear them say, "Oh, I'm doing fine—considering the alternative." And I ask myself and them as well: "But have you ever really considered the alternative?"

The alternative, of course, is life everlasting, eternal joy, life of unending union with God, a life where death and pain and anxiety will have no place. That's the alternative, and what's so bad about that?

I'm suggesting, dear friends, that in troubled times like these, we should be considering the alternative to life on earth, not that we want to rush off in that direction right now, but we should be finding peace and encouragement in our certain faith that a better life, far better, awaits each one of us. We should be considering the promised future to which each of us holds a claim—a faith claim, a title based on God's promise to us in Christ Jesus.

In troubled times like these, we should remind ourselves, as St. Paul reminded the Corinthians (1 Cor 2:9) that "eye has not seen, and ear has not heard, and what has not entered the human heart, what God has prepared for those who love him." The good life that will be yours forever is simply beyond imagining right now. But you should try to imagine it now and let that exercise serve to shore up your spirits, to build your confidence in these days of anxious uncertainty.

Notice how applicable to all this are the words from the Preface of Lent II: In this "great season of grace," that preface prayer in the old Roman Missal says, "You teach us how to live in this passing world with our heart set on the world that will never end." We're not counting on this world to pass out of existence anytime soon, but we do know that ours is a passing world. We do not expect ourselves to pass on from this life anytime soon, but we do know that we're not going to live forever and that someday we too shall pass. And we also know with the certainty that only faith can give, that God has prepared a place for us, and that we will be with God in that place forever. We also know that our happiness there is for us, at this moment, beyond all imagining. But we can count on it if we simply love God. Our faith assures us that God returns our love with life eternal.

17

Fourth Sunday of Lent

2 Chronicles 36:14–17, 19–23; Psalm 137;
Ephesians 2:4–10; John 3:14–21

GOD IS RICH IN MERCY

The opening words of the second reading, the excerpt from the Letter to the Ephesians, set the tone for our reflection on this Fourth Sunday of Lent; these words put a label on this liturgy: "God . . . is rich in mercy." God is indeed rich in mercy.

We have to believe that. We have to let those words sink deep into our consciousness. We have to let those words become a guiding principle for our lives. "God . . . is rich in mercy."

But we also know that God can be tough. We know that God can get angry. Just take another look at today's first reading from the Second Book of Chronicles. Priests and people had polluted the temple in Jerusalem with their infidelity. The Lord had compassion on them and sent his messengers to them, but they "mocked" the messengers and "despised" the Lord's warnings and "scoffed" at his prophets. And that was enough to stir up the Lord's anger to a point where he permitted the enemies of the people to destroy them.

But he also gave them a second chance through the positive intervention of King Cyrus of Persia. God's anger doesn't last. Our basic belief is that God is rich in mercy. That theme is introduced, as I said, in the second reading; it is then carried forward into the Gospel where we hear the reassuring, compelling, and truly beautiful words of Jesus spoken to Nicodemus and recorded for us by John: "For God so loved the world that he gave his only Son, so that everyone who believes in him might not perish but might have eternal life." The famous words of John 3:16: "God so loved the world." Think of the consequences of that love—for the world, for each one of us. "God did not send the Son into the world to condemn the world, but that the world might be saved though him."

How do you relate to the world? Do you love it? God did, and so should you. Love the world? Yes. And all that is in it? Yes.

Ignatius of Loyola, and the Ignatian spirituality that is his legacy to us, put a great emphasis on seeking and finding God in all things—seeking and eventually finding God, therefore, in the world. You don't have to flee the world to find God. God is there. God so loved the fallen world that he gave his only Son to buy it back, to redeem it after the fall of our first parents. That didn't happen right away. It took centuries until the "fullness of time" came about and the second person of the Blessed Trinity took flesh and came to dwell among us. What was at work all the while, however, what was alive and well in the world from the moment of the first great sin, the original sin, was God's love, God's mercy.

God is rich in mercy. And our merciful God so loved the world that he gave his only Son for the salvation of the world. And, as we know, the Son so loved us that he gave his life for us.

Note also that Jesus said to Nicodemus in the passage you heard today in the Gospel of John, "God did not send his Son into the world to condemn the world." Those are words worth pondering. Religion is all about love, not condemnation. It is possible for us to condemn ourselves by refusing God's love, by refusing to believe in Jesus whom God sent to save us. We are always free to do that. But that refusal is our action, not God's.

John, whose Gospel has a penchant for putting things in terms of light and darkness, explains our refusal this way: "And this is the verdict [the judgment]: that the light came into the world, but people preferred darkness to light, because their works were evil." Now you figure it out. How can it be that we choose darkness over light, that we prefer to dwell in darkness rather than enjoy the light? This is explainable only in terms of our "evil," which means our preference for sin over grace, hatred over love, self over salvation. We are capable of all this. That's why it is important to take Lent seriously. To take the opportunity Lent provides to check up on ourselves, indeed to check our evil impulses, to monitor our sinful tendencies so that we can refuse to let the downward pull of evil take us away from God.

Remember, it is not that the world is evil. There is evil in the world, yes, and we are capable of choosing evil, of preferring darkness to light. There's a mystery here that I cannot explain; I can simply point it out. But I can also point out that there is so much good in the world waiting to be discovered. There is much light beckoning you out of darkness. There are so many good things and good people waiting to help you find yourself and your path toward salvation. Pray that your Lenten abstentions and penance, your self-denial and self-control, will clarify your spiritual vision so that you can see the good that surrounds you in this world.

Perhaps the simplest and best takeaway for you today, in addition to the conviction that "God is rich in mercy," is a parallel conviction, as Psalm 33 puts it, that "The Lord…fills the earth with goodness." The goodness is there, for you, waiting to be found.

18

Fifth Sunday of Lent

Jeremiah 31:31–34; Psalm 51; Hebrews 5:7–9; John 12:20–33

THE GRAIN OF WHEAT

There is powerful imagery at work in today's Gospel.

In the agrarian culture that Jesus and his followers knew so well, the image of a wheat grain falling into the ground was a familiar one; it was natural for Jesus to employ this image in teaching a profound theological truth. Unless the wheat grain falls into the ground as if to die, Jesus explains, it remains alone, just a single grain of wheat; it remains alone—unfruitful, unproductive. But if it dies, it multiplies; it brings forth fruit.

This is a summary of the paschal mystery, the miraculous movement through death to life—the path Jesus will follow in his death and resurrection. Through death to life; through defeat to victory; through suffering on the cross to the glory of Easter. This riddle that we call the paschal mystery is made understandable by the down-to-earth (quite literally down-to-earth!) experience and example of a grain of wheat. There is a lesson here that speaks to one of life's most profound questions; it touches on the meaning of life as well as the mystery of the redemption of the whole human race.

Jesus prefaced this lesson by declaring that "The hour has come for the Son of Man [he was referring to himself] to be glorified." Notice, we are talking about glory here, although what looms immediately ahead for Jesus is defeat and death. Notice, too, that there is a lesson here that applies to the small, private, personal problems of failure and discouragement that we all encounter, as well as to the very large, eternally profound question of the salvation of the whole human race.

By uniting yourself with Christ today, the Christ who speaks to you of life *through* death, you can acquire an interpretive framework that will enable you to put personal problems in perspective; it will enable you to deal with disappointment and defeat, and stand strong in the face of any challenge life presents to you.

Listen again as Jesus speaks to you today:

> The hour has come for the Son of Man to be glorified. Amen, amen, I say to you, unless a grain of wheat falls to the ground and dies, it remains just a grain of wheat; but if it dies, it produces much fruit. Whoever loves his life, loses it, and whoever hates his life in this world will preserve it for eternal life. Whoever serves me must follow me, and where I am there also will my servant be. The Father will honor whoever serves me.

It might be helpful to take a moment to make sure we understand what Jesus means when he says that if you love your life, you will lose it, but if you "hate" your life in this world you will preserve it for life eternal. To "love" your life is a problem only if you permit your mind to be earthbound and self-enclosed, only if you shut God out of your life and close your heart to others. To "hate" your life in this world means to break out of self-enclosure, to detach yourself from self-love and self-will. It means not permitting yourself to be possessed by your possessions; it means "sitting loose" to the things of time, thus showing yourself to be fixed in the things of eternity.

And notice that it is in this context Jesus issued a call to follow him. Let that call be heard again by you today. He is always calling you. He never stops calling you. The call, of course, is to follow him. But, you may well be asking, where? Where is it that Christ wants me to go now? Who is it that Christ wants me to be or become?

"Whoever serves me, must follow me," says Jesus in this morning's Gospel. You want to serve him, I'm sure, but you may not be so sure about the how and where of your service. There is a time in your life when vocational choice is a major issue. You have to decide and you hope, by God's grace, that you will decide to be where God wants you to be and to do what God wants you to do. For most of you, however, that fundamental choice has been made and you are where God wants you to be—in married life, for example, or in a specific occupation or profession. The point for most of you today is to recognize anew that you are where you are by virtue of God calling you to be there. Capture once again at this moment your sense of vocation; savor it. Realize that you are not a random fluctuation in a field of vocational and occupational selection; know that you are where you are by the grace of God and doing what you do by God's grace also.

And realize that it is God's work, not yours that occupies your time. Pray, of course, that God will give success to the work of your hands, but realize that God is working within you and the results are his, not yours. The achievements are his. It is your privilege to be working along with God. Having an active sense of that reality can transform your working day. At a very minimum, it can convince you that you are not alone. God is there with you.

What about those of you who have yet to decide, who are trying to make important decisions that will shape your future? First, let me urge you to pray for light, for the grace of knowing what God wills for you. Next, I urge you to be generous, to be your own best self which means being the generous person God intended you to be. Then, from a platform of generosity, have the courage to take the plunge—to say yes to God and to the opportunity that may be presenting itself to you at this moment. It will take courage. You can never know for sure. You can never be absolutely certain that you are moving in the direction that God has in mind for you, that God knows to be best for you. You can never know for sure. But you can listen to your gut and follow your deep-down feelings and desires, and then take the plunge.

Confirmation will come your way by a deep-down sense of peace. You will feel that you are moving in the right direction. You may not be able fully to explain it to others, even to yourself, but you will just know and that knowledge will be enough for you. You will be at peace.

The hour has come for the Son of Man to be glorified. Amen, amen I say to you, unless a grain of wheat falls to the ground and dies, it remains just a grain of wheat; but if it dies, it produces much fruit. Whoever loves his life, loses it, and whoever hates his life in this world will preserve it for eternal life. Whoever serves me must follow me, and where I am there also will my servant be. The Father will honor whoever serves me.

There is a lesson there for all of you—the decided and the undecided. It is God who is calling. And only the generous should be thinking now about responding. Make your response, and peace will be yours.

19

Passion Sunday (Palm Sunday)

Isaiah 50:4–7; Psalm 22; Philippians 2:6–11; Mark 14:1—15:47

PALM SUNDAY—"HE EMPTIED HIMSELF"

After the annual proclamation of the Passion of the Lord, a homilist must take care to be attentive to an often-neglected wisdom principle, namely, that to add is to subtract. Let me simply attempt to extend this proclamation, as any homily should, by underscoring phrases from the first two readings from Scripture that were proclaimed by way of introduction to the passion narrative. These phrases can help connect you to the passion narrative and it to you in a personal way.

Isaiah told you in the opening reading that the Lord has given him "a well-trained tongue, that I might know how to speak to the weary a word that will rouse them." And among those words were these that fit so well on the lips of the Jesus you just followed on his Way of the Cross, words that apply to you in your weariness, in your effort to follow faithfully your Lord on your own way of the Cross: "The Lord God is my help, therefore I am not disgraced; I have set my face like flint, knowing that I shall not be put to shame."

Set your face like flint.

Believe that you shall never be disgraced if you follow him.

Know that you shall never be put to shame.

And the second reading—the Christological hymn in Paul's great Letter to the Philippians—tells you what you observed again this year with your mind's eye as you followed your Savior on his Way of the Cross. He "did not regard equality with God something to be grasped" ["to be clung to as a miser clings to his booty," in Joseph Fitzmyer's translation]. He didn't stand on rank or privilege; he didn't "lord it over" anyone.

"Rather," says St. Paul, "he emptied himself, taking the form of a slave, coming in human likeness; and found human in appearance, he humbled himself, becoming obedient to the point of death, even death on a cross."

He emptied himself.

He humbled himself.

And just because he did it for us all, is no reason not to say that he did it all for you, just for you.

He did it all for you.

He would have done it just for you, had no one else but you had need of salvation.

But the fact is we all stood in need of salvation. And all of us of all ages, all colors, all races, all nations, all times, all circumstances—all of us were saved by his Cross.

Living now, as we do, under the banner of the Cross, we must empty ourselves, humble ourselves, and open ourselves in gratitude to God who saved us in Christ. We show our gratitude by extending ourselves in grateful service to our brothers and sisters in the human community, our brothers and sisters for whom Christ suffered the indignities and death that the Passion according to Luke has helped us to recall.

IV
Triduum

. . . .

20

Holy Thursday, Mass of the Lord's Supper

Exodus 12:1–8, 11–14; Psalm 116;
1 Corinthians 11:23–26; John 13:1–15

BREAD BROKEN; CUP POURED OUT

At the Last Supper, Jesus said to his disciples, in effect: This is how I want you to remember me—as bread broken and passed around, as a cup poured out. And this is how I want all of you to relate to one another—as bread broken for the nourishment of others, as a cup poured out in generous service. Every priest has to ask himself whenever he celebrates the Eucharist, to what extent am I being broken and passed around for the nourishment of others? To what extent am I letting myself be poured out in generous service? To what extent is mine a "poured out" life?

And all who gather for the celebration of the Eucharist as we are assembled this evening for the Mass of the Lord's Supper, all of us who will receive communion together this evening, should be asking ourselves the exact same questions. Our attempt to give honest answers to those questions will inevitably open the door to questions of how we are living our lives, how faithful we are to the call to discipleship, how we are managing our wealth and property, how we are caring for or neglecting the poor and needy whom Jesus loved so dearly.

This same Jesus whom we remember tonight in the "breaking of the bread," promised to be present to us in a variety of ways, not least of which is his real presence in the Eucharist, which he instituted on the first Holy Thursday in what we now commemorate as the Mass of the Lord's Supper. It is worth asking ourselves at this moment, what does the "real presence" of Christ in the Eucharist really mean? And if it means anything at all, we have to ask ourselves at this moment in the history of the Church here in America, why are growing numbers of Catholics saying, in effect, "No thanks; not interested"? Why are fewer Catholics gathering on Sundays to remember their Lord in the breaking of the bread? Why are there not more of us here tonight to commemorate and celebrate the institution of the Eucharist on the first Holy Thursday?

It is worth recalling this evening that Christ is present to us in the eucharistic liturgy in four ways: (1) in his word—proclaimed from Scripture and reflected upon in the homily, (2) in his body and blood, (3) in the worshipping community (as Jesus said, "whenever two or three are gathered in my name, I'm there in their midst"), and (4) in the presence of the priest through whose ministry Christ now offers what he originally offered on the cross.

These four modes of Christ's presence in the eucharistic liturgy are, to say the least, insufficiently understood and vastly underappreciated in Catholic worshipping assemblies today. This four-way real presence should be a four-way stop sign halting the exodus that researchers are tracking and journalists are reporting when they observe the decline of participation, particularly among the young, in the Catholic Church today.

For the good of the Church, catechetical repair work is needed. Pastoral attention has to be paid to this problem. Priests, bishops, deacons, and lectors can "proclaim," but they and many others must also "explain" the four-way presence of Christ in the Eucharist. All of us share in that responsibility.

It takes faith, of course, to see Christ where only bread and wine are visible, but that's what faith does for the believer. It gives sight where vision fails.

Holy Thursday offers a special reminder that the sacrifice of the Mass is also a meal and worshippers have to attend to their role to gather around the table with their priest not as isolated worshippers but as brothers and sisters in the Lord who recognize Christ in one another as well as in the breaking of the bread.

So use your imagination to find a place for yourself tonight at the table of the Lord. Permit yourself to experience the attention you have received from the foot-washing Jesus. Feel the companionship of your fellow disciples there with you at the table of the Lord. And be grateful for the gift that is yours in the body and blood, soul and divinity of Jesus who is really present to you in the Eucharist that is yours this evening.

21

Good Friday, the Passion of the Lord

Isaiah 52:13–53; Psalm 31; Hebrews 4:14–16; 5:7–9; John 18:1–42

SIGN, CROSS, CRUCIFIXION

On this Good Friday, I invite you to consider (1) the crucifixion of Jesus, (2) the crucifix that we Catholic Christians venerate today and display in our homes and on the walls of our Catholic school class-rooms and Catholic hospital rooms, and (3) the Sign of the Cross that we trace on ourselves countless times throughout our lives. Let's take that third consideration first—the Sign of the Cross.

"In the name of the Father, and of the Son, and of the Holy Spirit." Those familiar words are said aloud or silently as the fingers of the right hand touch the forehead, move to the sternum or breastbone, and then cross from the left to right shoulder of the believer who seeks God's blessing or is initiating an experience of personal or communal prayer.

That external sign is there at the beginning of Mass. It introduces the so-called "grace" before meals. It initiates one's entrance into the sacrament of reconciliation. It sets one apart momentarily from the distractions and busyness of daily life for the experience of quiet prayer. The Sign of the Cross is a familiar and cherished part of Catholic life. Even when done hastily, perhaps casually and without much thought, the Sign of the Cross has special meaning for the believer.

Let me suggest a special dimension of that meaning for your con-sideration today. On Good Friday, you are painfully but gratefully aware that another body, not yours, hung on that cross on Calvary on the first Good Friday. Take a moment or two today, centuries removed as you now are from the first Good Friday, to recall that you, as a follower of Christ, a disciple of Jesus, are called to walk the Way of the Cross in your own day, in your own way, in your own corner of the world. You are called to participate in the repair work Jesus initiated, the work of reparation for sin—your personal sin and the sins of the world. Take a moment today to consider that, as St. Paul put it in the Letter to the Galatians (2:19–20): "I have been crucified with Christ; yet I live, no longer I, but Christ lives in me."

The Sign of the Cross, when you trace it on your own body, serves to remind that you too are crucified; you too hang there. By the grace of the living Christ, you hang there with him for the salvation of the world. Let the profound mystery of that reality sink deeper into your consciousness today.

And now look more closely at the crucifix that we Catholic Christians display in our homes, schools, hospitals, and many other places. It is there not as artwork to be admired; it is there to be venerated and to serve as a reminder of God's love—so great that God's Son became one of us, took our flesh, and gave his life for us on the cross so that we might have eternal life. The difference between the cross and the crucifix is the corpus—the body attached to the cross. That dead body rose again so that we might have life. We are not embarrassed by the spectacle of a bruised body—brutally beaten and hanging in death—wearing only a loincloth and exposed in full view. We are not embarrassed; we are profoundly grateful.

The crucifix says so much more than just a cross can say; the crucifix says death on the way to resurrection. Before the crucifix, all we can be is grateful.

And now let us consider together the historical fact of the crucifixion of Jesus. In the passion narrative you just listened to from the Fourth Gospel, you heard Jesus say: "Shall I not drink the cup that the Father gave me?" (John 18:11). He lived the poured out life—hidden for thirty years, public for three, and intensely painful for the brief days and hours immediately before his death. Good Friday reminds us that he was nailed to a cross and literally poured out his blood and last breath for us.

Few, if any of us, will ever have to experience the suffering he experienced. But each of us, in his or her own way and in the circumstances of his or her own life will experience some suffering that, in faith, we can unite with his for the salvation of the world.

On the walls of practically any Catholic church you may visit, you will find depictions of what we call the Stations of the Cross. For centuries believers have walked that way with Jesus in a devotional remembrance and representation of his final hours. Catholics participate in this devotional practice to give thanks and to gain strength— the strength they need to carry the "crosses" encountered in their transit through life.

Some years ago, I received a letter from an Immaculate Heart of Mary nun who was in a retirement community and infirmary as she neared the end of her vowed and religiously committed life. She knew I was a priest and said that although I did not know her, she wanted me to know that she had memories from her days as a young sister assigned to the parish where my widowed mother lived with her two preschool boys (my brother and me). This gracious lady wanted me to know that she cherished the memory of seeing my mother, with her toddler sons in tow, making the Stations of the Cross on Fridays during Lent in the parish church. I have no memory at all of this, but this nun said it shored up her vocational commitment to discipleship by seeing my mother devotionally renewing hers.

We all have "crosses" to bear and we can carry them more confidently (the word means "with faith") in the company of Veronica, Simon of Cyrene, and the other faithful followers of Jesus who accompanied Jesus on his Way of the Cross.

And don't forget Mary, the mother of Jesus, who stood there at the foot of the cross and to whom, as mother, Jesus committed his beloved disciple John and all his other disciples including you!

The crucifixion, the crucifix, and the Sign of the Cross. So much to consider. So much to be grateful for on this Good Friday.

22

Easter Vigil

Seven Old Testament Readings; Psalm 42;
Romans 6:3–11; Mark 16:1–7

"WHO WILL ROLL BACK THE STONE FOR US?"

Baptism quite obviously and quite properly dominates this Easter Vigil celebration. In song and sacrament, in water and word, baptism tonight touches us—all of us—heart and soul, mind and body.

Baptism symbolizes both the death and resurrection of Jesus. Baptism symbolizes for each one of us our death to sin, to the dead weight of the past, and our resurrection—our rising to new life in the Spirit.

Recall, if you will, that water possesses both a death-dealing and life-giving potential. Drowning is a possibility for those who are not careful; water can kill. Our life too depends on water: water to drink, water for bathing, water to irrigate our crop-producing fields, water to foster growth in our life-sustaining woodlands, grasslands, croplands; water to sustain all animal life. In the waters of baptism, we are plunged sacramentally and symbolically into the death of Jesus so that we too, by the power of God, may be raised with Jesus to walk in newness of life.

Unlike other sacraments, as for example Eucharist and reconciliation that are received often during the course of a lifetime, baptism is received only once. "We receive this saving baptism only once because there was only one death and one resurrection for the salvation of the world, and baptism is its symbol" (St. Basil).

Those who will be baptized tonight are breaking with the past and stepping onto a new path to the future. All the rest of us, who are repeating our baptismal vows tonight and recalling with thanks the gift of our own baptism, have these few graced moments to recall that a break with sin was made and a new life of grace begun in each of us. And in repeating our baptismal vows tonight, we have the opportunity to reflect on our progress on our faith journey and the quality of life that we are leading under the impact of grace and the love of the Holy Spirit within us, the grace and love that came to us in baptism.

Some of us who were long ago baptized may come here tonight with heavy hearts, with anxieties, with doubts, with a thousand distractions emerging from personal problems and our family and workplace responsibilities. Some of those who are to be baptized may perhaps be a bit anxious in face of the fact that a complete break with sin and the initiation of a new life of grace are now at hand.

Any or all of us could be in something of the agitated state that Mary Magdalene, Mary the mother of James, and the others who rushed out to the tomb found themselves on the first Easter. "Very early when the sun had risen, on the first day of the week," Mark's Gospel account tells us, "they came to the tomb. They were saying to one another, 'Who will roll back the stone for us from the entrance to the tomb?'"

Who will roll back the stone? In one way or another, any or all of us might be wondering at this moment: Who will roll back the stone of our doubt, of our guilt, of our anxiety and uncertainty; who will roll back the stone of discouragement and confusion? If you feel at all like that, then listen carefully to the next sentence in Mark's account of the first Easter: "When they looked up, they saw that the stone had been rolled back; it was very large."

When you look up tonight, when you look up to the God who raised Jesus from death to life, when you look up to the same God who raises us, through baptism, from death to life, and transforms us in the order of grace from death to life, from old to new, when you look up, simply believe that the stone of doubt, anxiety, worry, disbelief, guilt, discouragement, even apparent defeat, has been rolled away.

The early followers of Christ were, like you, worried about who would roll away the stone, and, "When they looked up, they saw that the stone had been rolled back." Beg for the grace tonight to celebrate the rolling back of your obstacles to resurrection, your stones, whatever their size or shape, whatever their origin.

Easter celebration may be a bit more difficult for us this year in the wake of death and destruction in Iraq. Iraq, as you know, is in the region once known as Mesopotamia, the birthplace of civilization six thousand years ago. The first traces of agriculture and trading are found there, the beginnings of organized religion, the development of mathematical methods, the flowering of the arts and architecture. The first form of writing and the beginnings of literature, including the first story of creation and the flood, originate there. Later civilizations were all influenced by Mesopotamia.

It was Mesopotamia, the land between the Tigris and the Euphrates Rivers, that was the location of the legendary Garden of Eden. The Middle East is a special place in our world; we use the expression "Holy Land" in reference to parts of that region. And so we are sad that death and destruction are in evidence there as we turn our minds and hearts to the celebration of Easter.

But now come forward with me to our modern times and look down with me to the earth beneath your feet, to the life that is yours, and to the corner of the earth that you occupy. Look to yourself and ask God for the grace of Easter faith that will enable you, as it enabled a man named Dan Sendzik, to become convinced of a practical, within-your-reach, non-miracle type of "resurrection" in your own life right now. I first saw these words forty years ago sewn or pasted onto a burlap banner hanging in the conference room of the original New York City office of the Christian Citizens' anti-hunger lobby Bread for the World. Dan Sendzik, an anti-hunger activist and BFW staffer, gave the banner by way of encouragement to Art Simon, founder of Bread for the World. Here are his words which I'm sure he would be pleased to have me share with you:

The rhythm of life is one of death and rebirth,
burial and resurrection,
of ending and beginning,
of closing down and opening up,
of bringing things to a halt and
of starting over again.
We stop being reborn only when we
stop wanting to.

Resurrection is impossible without enthusiasm,
and it is the possibility of resurrection that
excites enthusiasm.
To quit, to give up, is to die.
To try again, to start over, is to live.
We rise from the dead because we
want to. And the only barrier to
resurrection is quitting.

So let Easter enthusiasm fill your heart tonight as you pronounce or renew your baptismal vows, as you experience or witness these baptisms. Let us go forth from this Easter Vigil with a new commitment to life and with gratitude for both divine grace in our souls and new beginnings in our lives.

The stone has been rolled back for all of us. "We [can now] rise from the dead because we want to!"

V
Easter

. . . .

23

Easter Sunday

Acts 10:34, 37–43; Psalm 118; Colossians 3:14;
John 20:1–9 or Mark 16:1–8

PETER ATE AND DRANK WITH HIM

In today's reading from the Acts of the Apostles, Peter establishes his credentials as a witness to the risen Christ by saying that he "ate and drank" with Jesus after Jesus returned to life from death on the cross. There is something about eating and drinking with another person that puts one on a practical level of believability. Peter didn't simply say he saw Jesus, or that he talked to him, or that others told him that they had seen Jesus. No, he said he had real down-to-earth contact with Jesus. He ate and drank with him. Ghosts do not eat and drink. Jesus is really alive; he has truly risen. Peter knows, and therefore Peter is a reliable witness.

You enjoy eating and drinking companionship with others every day. And if you mention to someone that you ate and drank with someone else whom they know, they have every reason to believe that the other person is alive and well and in circulation. That's exactly the point Peter wanted to make. Shortly after Jesus died on the cross, the power of God made him alive and well again and put him back in circulation—a new kind of circulation, to be sure, we call it the risen life, but a seeable, touchable circulation that is real. And if you accept the witness of Peter, if you believe that Jesus died and rose again, you will, as Peter put it, "receive forgiveness of sins through his name." So it is important that there be witnesses, like Peter, to the resurrection so that others might believe and, believing, gain eternal life.

The Liturgy of the Word on this Easter Sunday invites all of us to believe—to renew and deepen our belief in the risen Lord—and the reality that we celebrate today invites us all to become witnesses in our own time and in our own way to the risen Christ. Our lives, as disciples of Christ, should witness to the reality of the resurrection. That can be done in a variety of ways, but the way I would offer for your consideration today is the simple eating-and-drinking style of witness. You eat and drink with others every day. I'm suggesting that those others can see in you some of the values Jesus embodied, some of the lessons Jesus taught. So much of what Jesus said and did was ordinary. True, the miraculous and truly extraordinary event of the resurrection brought him back to life, but the life to which he returned is the eating-and-drinking kind of ordinary life that you live every day. In you—leading that life every day—others can see Jesus. They can see the kind, caring, thoughtful, generous Jesus in you, in your kindness, your caring, your thoughtfulness, your generosity. Peter was, as I said, a reliable witness. How reliable are you, how reliable am I in witnessing to the risen Jesus?

We don't have to talk about it all the time. We just have to believe and live as if we did indeed believe. Our lives, as believers, will be qualitatively different from the lives of those who have no faith—those who, even if they heard, do not yet believe. The problem of unbelief is an enormous one in our day—these many centuries after the fact of the resurrection. We cannot be content not to do anything about it. But doing something about it does not necessarily mean preaching or even persuading. It does, however, mean living our ordinary lives—our eating-and-drinking existence—differently because of the resurrection.

It first means living gratefully. How can we not be grateful for the gift of faith that came to us through the death and resurrection of Jesus? And how can we contemporary Catholics, who no longer show up for Mass on Sundays, have missed the obvious connection between the Holy Thursday institution of the Eucharist and the Easter Sunday resurrection? We live gratefully because we've been redeemed by the life, death, and resurrection of Jesus. We show our gratitude liturgically—that is, we declare ourselves to be "much obliged"—every Sunday, and Sunday is Resurrection Day, the first day of the week when we give our thanks in the celebration of the Eucharist.

And those with whom we eat and drink on any day of the week, those who see us living gratefully in our ordinary daily lives, will see something not just different, but something enormously attractive, and they might—just might, by the grace of God—begin to think about that difference and wonder why. When that happens, we are witnessing, just as Peter witnessed, to the resurrection.

The very thought of being or becoming an ingrate is both frightening and abhorrent when introduced into this Easter consideration. As believers, we have learned the resurrection lesson that "death's not what we're moving toward; it's what we're coming from!"

Ingrates no more, all we can be is grateful as we walk away now from this Holy Week Triduum more determined than ever to live gratefully every day of the year.

24

Second Sunday of Easter

Acts 4:32–35; Psalm 118; 1 John 5:1–6; John 20:19–31

PEACE BE WITH YOU!

"Jesus came and stood in their midst and said to them, 'Peace be with you'" (John 20:19). Let that encounter happen right here, right now, for you, my friends. Reimagine the appearance of Jesus to his disciples, but put yourself in that circle of disciples and bring the meeting forward to this present day. Let your mind's eye see Jesus—the victorious, risen Jesus of glory—stand before you and say to you: "Peace be with you."

Hear the words. Let them sink into your soul. Hear him and believe that his farewell gift of peace is yours to accept, if you want it. In order to prepare yourself to receive Christ's farewell gift of peace, all you need is faith. You already possess the gift of faith; all you need to do now is let your faith become more consciously yours.

Faith is like a flame hidden in a bed of embers. It is there. It needs a breeze, a fan of some sort to move over the bed of embers so that the flame of conscious faith can rise. Faith is a gentle but flaming awareness of God's presence in you, with you, for you, especially when difficulties and doubts may press in upon you. Doubt—you meet the famous "doubting Thomas" in today's Gospel account—doubt does not disqualify any one of you from the community of believers. To live is to doubt. To live in peace with your doubts, to become stronger in and through your doubts, is Christ's Easter gift to you. Take it today. He presents this Easter gift with the words: "Peace be with you. As the Father has sent me, so I send you" (John 20:21). Indeed, he does send each one of you as an ambassador of his peace, as a witness to his word, as a believer, a follower, a disciple. And all he asks of you is to believe, to be faithful.

You may have noticed in the second reading, the selection from the First Letter of John, this sentence: "And the victory that conquers the world is our faith." Your faith makes you, like Christ, a victor. Your faith prepares your soul for the gift of peace. And gifted with peace within, you are invited to go out and witness to that peace by living your faith.

Thomas was not present when Jesus, after rising from the dead, first met with his circle of disciples and offered them the gift of peace. One week later, Thomas who had expressed his doubts and made it clear that he needed evidence before he would "believe"; one week later Thomas is there. The doors are closed and Jesus miraculously appears in their midst and says again: "Peace be with you." And he invites Thomas quite literally to poke through the evidence and, after the probing, to "not be unbelieving, but believe" (John 20:27).

Thomas responds with the famous exclamation that has come down to us through the centuries as an appropriate response to the reception of holy communion, "My Lord and my God" (John 20:28).

Yes indeed, it is God whom you encounter today in prayer and sacrament. This is the one, the Holy One, the victorious Christ whom you can now touch and cling to only with the embrace of faith, not with the tangible contact that the doubting Thomas required. And because those tangible contacts are not available to you these many centuries later, you qualify to be numbered among those Jesus had in mind when he said in the presence of Thomas and the others: "Blessed are those who have not seen and have believed" (John 20:29). That includes, of course, each one of us! We are especially and remarkably blessed. We have not seen but we do believe!

Relish the thought. You are "blessed." Jesus said so. And what does Jesus want you to have as a sign of this blessedness? Peace.

Throughout these early encounters with his disciples—remember they were the ones who fled, who abandoned him in his sufferings; they are the ones who hesitated, hid, denied, doubted—they are the very ones to whom he says, "Peace be with you," deep, abiding, lasting peace be with you. So don't ever become convinced that your doubts, denials, hesitations, or moments of cowardice are disqualifying. You can still believe. You can still enjoy the gift of peace. You share with

Jesus in his victory. As John the Evangelist said so well, "the victory that conquers the world is our faith."

What is it that faith brings into your life? How does faith set you apart from those who have no faith as you go about your daily activity? In practical terms, how might faith make you different? I think the answer to that is persistence or perseverance. The person of faith will persist. The person of faith will weather the storms. A person motivated by faith will be a better person over time, over the long haul. The parent who has religious faith will stick with parenting responsibilities in good times and in bad. The teacher, manager, lawyer, health care provider will, if he or she is a person of faith, believe that God is there in the work, that God is served by the work, and his or her persistence in the work will produce a better teacher, manager, lawyer, health care provider, and the same holds true for any occupation followed in faith and blessed with the gift of peace.

Peace is no small gift, and it is yours. Nor is faith an insignificant gift, and faith is yours. As we pray for peace in our world, particularly in the Middle East, be mindful of the wise dictum attributed to St. Thomas More: Don't pray for anything that you are unwilling to work for. Not that your work alone will make it happen, but don't expect it to happen without your willingness to work.

"If you want peace, work for justice," said Pope Paul VI decades ago. Perhaps we do not yet have peace because we have not been working hard enough for justice.

In the context and vocabulary of today's readings, let me suggest that if you want the peace that Jesus offers when he says, "Peace be with you," if you want the peace that Jesus holds out to you, take a moment to examine the quality of your faith. Not the quantity of your faith; faith is unquantifiable. But look to the quality of your faith— your readiness to let go, to trust, to entrust yourself to God. A window on the quality of your faith in this Easter season is the sense you may or may not have at this moment that Jesus is victorious, that his victory is your victory, and it is not that you have picked a winner in choosing to follow Christ, but that a winner has clearly and certainly picked you!

Relish that thought. Celebrate that victory. And enjoy the peace that your acceptance, in faith, of that victory surely brings.

25

Third Sunday of Easter

Acts 3:13–15, 17–19; Psalm 4; 1 John 2:1–5a; Luke 24:35–48

FIRST COMMUNION SUNDAY

A portion of the opening sentence in today's Gospel reading offers a nice keynote for a homily on this first communion weekend. Let me repeat the words: "Jesus was made known to them in the breaking of bread."

The breaking of the bread.

We are bread breakers, we Catholic Christians. We remember the Lord in the breaking of the bread. That means we get a glimpse of what Christ was like in what we call "holy communion," and in that glimpse we find a clue to the kind of persons we ought to be, we believers who eat his body and drink his blood in the sacrament we call holy communion.

What do I mean when I say we catch a glimpse of what Christ was like when we break the eucharistic bread together? Well, it is as if Jesus said to his disciples on the night before he died, the night of what we remember as the "Last Supper," it is as if he said, "This is how I want you to remember me—as bread broken and passed around for the nourishment of others, as a cup poured out for others." The generous, courageous, self-sacrificing Jesus is like bread broken, like a cup poured out. You will recognize these as signs of love. They point to a good and generous person, to one who sacrificed his life for your salvation.

And in catching this glimpse in these sacramental signs of what Jesus was like when he walked among us, we also get a look at what the persons who follow Jesus are called to be—generous and self-sacrificing in the service of others. Like bread broken; like a cup poured out. No thought given to gathering up the pieces and remaking the loaf and taking it back; no thought given to recouping the contents of the cup. No. Christ gave himself with no thought of pulling back. We, who feed upon Christ and thus draw our strength from him, are to give ourselves in loving service to one another as our way of thanking God and showing our love for God by demonstrating love for one another.

Did you ever notice that there is no children's table here at the Table of the Lord? You probably remember having a children's table at home on special days like Thanksgiving and Christmas and other special occasions when you had company and a special smaller table was set up to the side for the children. Well, you cannot come to this holy communion meal, you cannot take a place at this eucharistic table, unless you are big enough to believe. Not to understand fully, because no mere human can understand fully this mystery of God's gift to us in holy communion, but big enough to make an act of faith.

This is what we believe about holy communion. We believe that when the priest takes into his hands ordinary bread and ordinary wine and says the words Jesus spoke over ordinary bread and wine at the Last Supper, when the words, "This is my body; this is my blood" are spoken over bread and wine at the altar, then what was a moment before just bread and wine becomes the body and blood of Jesus. That's what we believe. Jesus Christ is there, whole and entire, soul and divinity, under the appearance, under the sacramental signs of bread and wine. That's what we believe. That's why we adore the consecrated host, the blessed cup. That's why we genuflect. That's why we receive this eucharistic meal with reverence and dignity.

Now there's another startling truth that we believe about this special meal, this holy communion. Unlike ordinary meals where what you eat becomes part of you (and we all know that if we eat too much there is soon more of us on the bathroom scale than we want to see there!); unlike ordinary eating, when we partake of this holy meal we become what we eat! By that I mean, we are divinized; this nourishment gives us the very life of Christ. We become what we eat.

And another startling truth about this sacramental reality of holy communion is this. In ordinary meals that we share with others, even in a pizza party snack that we share with other friends, each of us has our own portion, just a part or portion of the meal. We share the meal by dividing it up into portions. But in this sacramental meal, each of us receives an identical portion. Sure, you receive a separate host, a separate part of the one bread and a separate sip from the one cup, but what you receive, what you share with others at this table, is exactly the same, the identical portion of the eucharistic meal, because what you and the person next to you, and those before and after you in the communion line, what each of you receives is the same Jesus Christ, the body and blood of Jesus. And that's why we call this communion "holy com-union," because you are united with, you are in union with, everyone else anywhere and everywhere in the world who receives the body and blood of Christ in this same sacrament.

The pope in St. Peter's in Rome, and you here in this church, receive the same portion of this eucharistic meal. The Chaldean Catholic and the American soldier in Iraq receive the same portion of this eucharistic meal even if they happen to be at different Masses in Baghdad. Men and women, rich and poor, whose skin color may be black, white, brown, or yellow, whenever and wherever they approach the communion table, are receiving identical nourishment that they cannot receive worthily if they hold hatred in their hearts for those of other skin colors, other ethnic identification, other social class.

These are wonderful truths that require a certain age of reason in order to believe. That's why there is no children's table at the Eucharist. In holy communion, whether it be one's first or twenty-thousandth reception of this sacrament, in holy communion we grow together in love. We come to the table reconciled to our neighbor. And at this table we receive what an ancient Christian writer called the "medicine of immortality." For the food we take at this table nourishes us for eternal life.

Back now to the opening words of today's Gospel story. "The two disciples recounted what had taken place on the way, and how Jesus was made known to them in the breaking of the bread."

That's the very end of the story of the two disciples on the road to Emmaus that you find in the twenty-fourth chapter of Luke's Gospel. It is after the death and burial of their leader, the Jesus they followed for three years, but abandoned when he was arrested, tried, scourged, and crucified. They had fled; they were deserters. They then heard stories of his return to life, but they were confused. They still did not have the gift of Easter faith.

They are two sad sacks on the road to Emmaus, walking along in dejection when a stranger falls into step with them and starts telling them about the events that happened the last few days in Jerusalem, and how this man Jesus had really been teaching anyone who wanted to listen the revelation that God had started pouring out through the voices of the prophets and great teachers centuries earlier.

The two disciples did not realize it was Jesus who fell into step and was walking along with them. It was evening when the three travelers reached the town of Emmaus and the original two begged this stranger to stay with them. At table, the stranger took bread, and broke it, and gave it to them, and it was at that moment that they recognized him— in the breaking of the bread. Their hearts "burned within them," Scripture tells us, at that moment.

May your hearts burn within you as you recognize today your Lord and Savior Jesus in the breaking of the bread, which is for some blessed children today their first, but for all who approach this table at any Mass a special encounter, a truly holy communion.

26

Fourth Sunday of Easter

Acts 4:8–12; Psalm 118; 1 John 3:1–2; John 10:11–18

A GOOD SHEPHERD LAYS DOWN HIS LIFE FOR HIS SHEEP

There are four key considerations to focus on this morning: (1) Good Shepherd Sunday, (2) Mother's Day, (3) first holy communion for these children gathered around the altar, and (4) the fact that next Sunday a special collection will be taken up for Catholic Relief Services, the overseas assistance program sponsored by the Roman Catholic Bishops of the United States.

- The Good Shepherd—the Gospel portrayal we have of Jesus as shepherd, the flesh and blood friend we have in Jesus who, like a good shepherd, laid down his life for us.
- Mother's Day—a day to honor your mother, to give thanks to God for the mother who brought you to birth and nurtured you through years of development.
- A special collection for Catholic Relief Services is coming up. As we celebrate first reception of the bread of life, we should remind ourselves that whenever we receive the bread of life, we should do something to help the poor receive the bread *for life.*
- First communion—first reception of the bread of life.

In holy communion, you receive the body and blood of your good friend, Jesus. By eating his flesh and drinking his blood, as you do in holy communion, you gain the strength you need to be like Jesus, to be gentle enough to care like a shepherd for others, and to be strong enough and courageous enough to lay down your life for others, as Jesus laid down his life for you. And on Mother's Day you have a special moment to think of that gracious and loving lady who has given so generously of herself for you. Finally, by contributing to the special overseas relief collection next weekend, you are adopting a practice that all of us should associate with the reception of holy communion, namely that whenever we receive the bread of life, we should seriously consider our obligation as Christians to share the bread *for* life with those who are less fortunate than we.

So this is indeed a special four-point celebration today!

Let me point out to you first communicants today that there is no children's table here at the meal we are about to share together. Did you notice that? Do you remember having a children's table at home on big days like Thanksgiving and Christmas? Well there is no children's table at church because you have to be big enough to believe before you can take a place at this table. You have to be big enough to believe (not fully and completely understand, just big enough to believe) that this is very special food that you are about to receive. Let me tell you how special it is.

We believe that under the signs of bread and wine, we receive the body and blood of Jesus in holy communion. When the priest says the words over ordinary bread and wine, the same words that Jesus said over ordinary bread and wine at the Last Supper, we believe that the ordinary bread and wine become the body and blood of Christ. We believe it because Jesus said so. We know that it still looks and tastes like ordinary bread and wine, but we believe that it is no longer ordinary; it is the body and blood of Christ. And so we bow, we adore, and we can say as Thomas said when he saw Jesus in the upper room after the resurrection, "My Lord and My God!" But there's more to it than that.

We also believe that, unlike ordinary food, which becomes part of us when we eat it, we believe that we become part of what we eat when we receive holy communion. By that I mean we become more like Christ when we consume his body and blood; we become what we eat; we become divinized through our reception of holy communion.

Another remarkable thing we believe about holy communion is that each of us receives not a share but the identical portion of this meal.

Each of us receives the body and blood, soul and divinity of the same Jesus Christ who gave himself up for us. When you receive holy communion, you receive the same portion that the pope received this morning when he celebrated Mass. You receive the same portion that the Chaldean Catholic in Iraq, as well as the American soldier in Iraq, received this morning at Mass on the other side of the world. You receive the same portion that any other believer—black, white, brown, or yellow skin; rich or poor; regardless of national origin or any other difference—the portion for each is the same for all. Why? Because it is the one body and one cup that Christ gave for us, for our nourishment, for our salvation. So, we cannot exclude others from our friendship because of skin color or national origin and still approach this table in good faith and receive the Lord worthily.

When the Lord Jesus gathered his disciples around the table of the Last Supper for the very first holy communion, he took bread and broke it; he passed the cup around, and he said, in effect, this is how I want you to remember me—like bread broken and passed around for the nourishment of others, like a cup poured out in generous self-giving for others. Remember me that way. If you want to be like me, break yourselves open in service of others, pass yourself around for the benefit of others. Isn't that a great way of describing our Good Shepherd who was generous enough to lay down his life for us?

And isn't that what good Christian mothers try to do? Isn't that what your mother did for you? How can we be anything but grateful today on Mother's Day, First Communion Day, and Good Shepherd Sunday?

So welcome to the table of the Lord, my young friends who will soon bring up the gifts and set the table and not only receive holy communion for the first time, but lead your parents up here as well. And we not only pray a prayer of thanks that you have come to this day, we offer you congratulations that you are now big enough to believe and take the place that has been reserved for you at the table of the Lord.

27

Fifth Sunday of Easter

Acts 9:26–31; Psalm 22; 1 John 3:18–24; John 15:1–8

"I AM THE VINE, YOU ARE THE BRANCHES"

This Gospel story is a good one to reflect on at this Mass—a first holy communion Mass—during which we welcome these wonderful children to the table of the Lord.

I first want to ask these children to think back to big holidays and family dinners at home—Thanksgiving, Christmas—days when a lot of relatives are invited to sit down together to enjoy a great meal. Now did any of you, when you were smaller, sit at a "children's table?" Was there a table off to the side for the kids?

Well, did you ever notice that there is no children's table here in church, here by the table of the Lord? The reason we have no children's table here is because you have to be big enough to believe that this is special food before you can participate in this meal. You have to be big enough to believe, not necessarily to understand fully, just to believe that this is special food—the body and blood of Jesus under the appearance of bread and wine.

Faith means taking something on the authority of another and believing it to be true, even if we have no direct proof, only the word of another. In this case we have the word of Jesus who tells us that his flesh, which comes to us under the appearance of bread, is real food; and his blood under the appearance of wine, is real drink. Jesus says, anyone who eats my flesh and drinks my blood will have eternal life and happiness with me forever in heaven.

You remember, don't you, that at the Last Supper, when Jesus and his special friends were at table together, he took bread, and broke it, and gave it to them saying, "This is my body." And he took the cup filled with wine and blessed it and said, "This is my blood." And then he told them that after he was gone, they should to do the same thing, saying those same words, in remembrance of him. That was the beginning of the first Mass (which was completed by the sacrifice on Calvary the very next day). That's what we repeat here at this altar, this table, every Sunday. But you have to be big enough to believe before you can have a place at this table.

Did you hear the words of Jesus in the Gospel story about the vine and the branches. He said, "I am the true vine....Remain in me, as I remain in you. Just as a branch cannot bear fruit on its own unless it remains on the vine, so neither can you unless you remain in me. I am the vine, you are the branches" (John 15:1, 4–5). Now think about that. Think of a vine, or think of the main trunk of a tree. And notice how the branches shoot out from the trunk, from the vine. Can you tell exactly where it is that the vine ends and the branch begins? Isn't Jesus making the point that the same life runs through both vine and branch? In vines and tree trunks, we call that life-giving substance sap. When Christ is the vine and we are the branches, we call that life-giving reality grace—divine grace, divine life and love within us. Why within us? Because we are joined to Christ as a branch is part of a tree.

That's why Jesus can say to you, "Whoever remains in me and I in him [or her], will bear much fruit, because without me you can do nothing" (John 15:5). It is so important not to cut yourself off from Christ. It is so necessary to participate in his life because without that life, "you can do nothing."

Holy communion is food that nourishes the divine life within you. Now let me tell you a couple of interesting facts that we take on faith about this special food. First, as I said, it is the body and blood of Christ. When the priest at the altar says the words that Jesus spoke over ordinary bread and wine at the Last Supper, when the priest says over bread and wine here at the altar, "This is my body; this is my blood," that ordinary bread and wine, retaining their appearance, become the body and blood of Jesus.

Second, unlike the ordinary food that you eat every day, this food does not become part of you; you become part of it. You become like

Christ. You become divinized. The divine life of Christ the vine, the tree trunk, so to speak, is the same life that flows into you, the branch.

And another difference between this special food and the regular food you have at meals every day is this: In holy communion, you receive the exact same portion that the others at the table of the Lord receive. You receive today the same portion that the pope received when he celebrated Mass this morning. You receive the same portion that the Chinese Catholic received today at Mass, the same portion the African Catholic receives. You don't just have a share, as you would if you were cutting up a pizza and passing it around, no, in this meal you receive the exact same portion that others receive because this is the one bread, the one cup that Jesus gives for the nourishment of us all.

So if you want to receive this holy communion worthily, you cannot separate yourself from others because of their national origin, skin color, economic status; you can't think of yourself as better than others who receive the same portion that you receive at this eucharistic meal.

When Jesus took bread at the Last Supper and broke it and gave it to those friends of his gathered there with him, he said, this is how I want you to remember me, as bread broken and passed around for the nourishment of others. That's what I want you to be, because you believe in me. I want you to be bread broken and passed around for the nourishment of others in the human community.

You may have heard the announcement at the beginning of Mass that a special second collection is being taken up today for Catholic Relief Services, a special collection to help the poor overseas. So when the children bring up the Offertory gifts, you will see them bring up a basket of food that will be given to the poor. All of us, whether we are making our first communion today or made our first communion years ago, all of us should remember to try to share the bread *for* life whenever we receive the bread of life. Today's second collection gives all the big folks here a chance to do just that.

So happy First Communion Day to you children up front here. You will soon set the altar. You will soon receive your Lord. When I say the "body of Christ," you will say "Amen," meaning indeed it is; I do believe that this is "my Lord and my God." Your friend Jesus will be happy to be with you, to live within you, and to work with you to make this a better world. Blessings on you all!

28

Sixth Sunday of Easter

Acts 10:25–26, 34–35, 44–48; Psalm 98; 1 John 4:7–10; John 15:9–17

"BELOVED, LET US LOVE ONE ANOTHER"

If I were to rename this homily, I think I'd call it "Raising the Bar." You know what that means. I guess it originated in track and field competition—raising the high jump bar, raising the bar that pole-vaulters have to clear, making the high hurdles higher and higher. Maybe the phrase has its origin elsewhere; I really don't know. But whenever you hear it, you know what it means: higher standards, greater performance expectations.

Well Jesus raises the bar for all of us in the segment of his farewell discourse that you heard in today's Gospel reading. "Jesus said to his disciples . . . 'This is my commandment: love one another as I love you.'"

"As I love you," he says to them on the night before he died; that's the way you should love one another. "As I have loved you," he says to each of us these many centuries later. "Love one another, as I have loved you." How is that raising the bar?

Notice it is Jesus the priest at the first Mass, at the Last Supper on the night before he died giving his disciples a new commandment. "This is my commandment: love one another as I love you. No one has greater love than this, to lay down one's life for one's friends." Notice this is a new commandment. The bar is going up.

What was the old commandment? Well Jesus the rabbi, the teacher, during his public life, on one of his itinerant preaching journeys, was asked by someone: "Teacher, which commandment in the law is the greatest?" (Matt 22:36), referring, of course, to the Law of Moses, the Law that Jesus on the night before he died turned into the old Law. In response to this question about the greatest commandment, Jesus the rabbi, the teacher, dutifully and faithfully quoted the Law and said: "You shall love the Lord, your God, with all your heart, with all your soul, and with all your mind. This is the greatest and the first commandment. The second is like it: You shall love your neighbor as yourself" (Matt 22:37–39).

Those words are familiar to you all. In fact, they've been translated or transposed for you into the Golden Rule: "Do unto others as you would have them do unto you." They've been the basis for an ethic of reciprocity that sets a pretty high standard for all of us. Love one another as you love yourself. Do unto others as you would have them do unto you. Fairly high performance standard, you might say. A high goal. You may fall short, but you've got your eye on that goal. Reaching it on a habitual basis would be, you might say, a high level of Christian perfection. Trouble is, that goal was put in place, that bar was set, before Christ came, before there was a Christian religion. Before there was anything that could be called "Christian perfection."

So along comes Christ and he raises the bar. He announces a new commandment. He commands us (who would be his followers, who would call ourselves "Christian"), he tells us we must love one another as he has loved us, to the point, therefore, of laying down our lives for one another. He calls upon us, indeed commands us, not to be content with an ethic of reciprocity—doing to others as we would have them do unto us, loving others as we love ourselves. No, he calls us to an ethic of renunciation, to put others first and ourselves second, to love one another as he has loved us. And that means sacrifice. That means striving toward the "no greater love" goal enunciated by Jesus in the Gospel selection you heard today: "No one has greater love than this, to lay down one's life for one's friends."

Now we have to be realistic and practical about this. We're not talking about running into the burning building and rescuing the trapped child. We're not talking about jumping into the icy waters and saving the drowning man. Those would, of course, be splendid examples of self-sacrificing love. But we're talking about daily Christian living, about laying our lives down day by day for one another, particularly those closest to us, those within our reach: spouse, children, parents, relatives, neighbors, coworkers, fellow parishioners, those who break bread with us at this eucharistic table.

We can't come to this table worthily if we withhold love, kindness, courtesy, consideration for others. We can't call ourselves Christians if we are unwilling to be helpful, patient, kind to one another. That's what it means to lay down your life for another day by day in fidelity to the new Christian commandment of love. "Love one another as I have loved you."

Let it happen in families, in the workplace, here in our worshipping community. Let it happen wherever you walk, whenever you talk, at whatever point you happen to be on your faith journey. "Love one another as I have loved you."

This Gospel selection is a favorite for wedding liturgies. You may have heard it at your own wedding ceremony. It is good for married people, or people about to be married, to think of marriage as a perfect setting for living out this new commandment day by day. Within marriage, you can enter into a holy competition to outdo one another in moving toward that "no greater love" goal. In meeting the responsibilities of spousal and parental love, anyone who has been there knows that there are endless opportunities to imitate the self-sacrificing love of Christ, to love one another as Christ loved you.

That's why the Church in its wisdom has been saying for centuries to couples about to pronounce their marriage vows to "let the security of your wedded life rest on the great principle of self-sacrifice.... Sacrifice is usually difficult and irksome but love can make it easy and perfect love can make it a joy."

There's a lesson there for all of us, married or single, whatever our circumstances may be, wherever our Christian vocation may take us. And the lesson is this: love is sacrifice; sacrifice is love. Live that kind of love and you'll know happiness. If all of us live that kind of love, self-sacrificing love, we'll be living out the new commandment and the world in which we live will be an unimaginably better place.

29

Ascension

Acts 1:1–11; Psalm 47; Ephesians 1:17–23; Mark 16:15–20

"KNOW THAT I AM WITH YOU ALWAYS"

You have an ascension "keepsake" here in today's Gospel reading from Mark. Jesus said, just before departing from his disciples and ascending into heaven, "Know that I am with you always, until the end of the world!" That's a promise. That promise was made to each one of you by someone who cannot be anything but faithful to his promises. You can count on it. And you should think of it not only when you make the ascension meditation during your recitation of the glorious mysteries of the Rosary; you should think of it every day. "Know that I am with you always, until the end of the world."

What does it mean to you to be accompanied by the risen Lord every day of your life? As a child, you may have been taught that you have a guardian angel at your side in your journey through life, and no doubt you found that comforting. But how much more reassuring it should be to know that you have the risen Christ there with you as well.

Confusion, uncertainty, anxiety, fear, temptation—none of these is a stranger to you in your lived experience of the journey of faith in this world. But because it is a journey of faith, you believe that Jesus is there with you every inch of the way. What a pity it is to forget this. What a loss it is to deprive yourself of the strength of knowing that you are not walking alone. You are not an isolated sojourner. You are always with the Lord. He will be there for you and every believer until the end of the world.

This ascension liturgy provides you with a few moments of reflection for a reality check. This is indeed the reality. The risen Christ is with you regardless of your awareness or consciousness of this fact at any given moment. Naturally, you cannot be thinking of this fact at every moment of the day. You are busy about many things. But you can and should pause from time to time to remind yourself that you have an ascension promise from your risen and ascended Lord who is now in heaven, but who promised also to be with you on earth and he remains faithful to that promise.

So why should you be unsettled? Why should you not be at peace? If you are trying to do your best, if you are trying to be faithful to the Lord's commandments, if you really want to align your own free will with the will of God, you should regard any unsettlement or absence of peace as a temptation from Satan, the enemy of human nature. Just say, as Jesus said, "Be gone Satan!" (Matt 4:10). There are devils at work in the world. Jesus told us that this would be the case. There will be temptations in your life; this is no cause for surprise. But if you are doing your best to make progress in your journey toward heaven, any discouragement that troubles you is not coming from the Lord, it is the work of the enemy of your human nature who wants to sidetrack you from following Christ. If, on the other hand, there is peace—not complacency, but peace—in your heart as you move forward in the following of Christ, that peace is from God who wants you to stay on track.

That's what today's readings invite you to do—stay on track in your faith journey with the risen and ascended Lord. Those early disciples who stood there and watched as he departed from them to ascend into heaven, they had memories of their companionship with him on earth. The Gospels provide you with a book of memories, too. Cherish them. Pray over them. Let them work within you to acquaint you with the kind of person it is who promised to be with you until the end of the world.

God wants you to cherish and savor those memories. This, I think, is what Paul had in mind when he said to the Ephesians in today's second reading: "May the God of our Lord Jesus Christ, the Father of glory, grant you a spirit of wisdom and insight to know him clearly. May he enlighten your innermost vision that you may know the great hope to which he has called you."

The ascension reflection that I am recommending to you today will indeed sharpen your innermost vision and bring you great hope. What more do you need to continue on in your journey of faith with the ascended Lord who promised to be with you always?

30

Seventh Sunday of Easter

Acts 1:15–17, 20–26; Psalm 103; 1 John 4:11–16; John 17:11–19

"I DO NOT ASK THAT YOU TAKE THEM OUT OF THE WORLD"

There is a line in the high priestly prayer of Jesus, part of today's Gospel reading—spoken by Jesus to the Father by way of intercession for those he would leave behind to follow him on earth—a line that speaks to the secular vocation of the Christian in the world. It is a line that suggests a link between the life of faith and the life of work. It is a divinely inspired line that presents you with an opportunity to reflect today on your call to be in, but not of, the world; to work in the secular city for the glory of God and the good of others. You are called to work out your own salvation, with God's help, in a world where you need protection from "the evil one." And so the line that invites your reflection today is this: "I do not ask that you take them out of the world but that you keep them from the evil one."

Your faith journey does not remove you from the world. Your faith journey makes your transit through this world meaningful. Faith gives meaning to your life. You believe that you are created by God. You believe that you are redeemed by the death, resurrection, and ascension of Jesus Christ. You believe that you have divine life within you— we call it grace. You believe that you are called—that is, you have a vocation—to follow Christ. And you believe that you are called specifically to motherhood or fatherhood, or to unmarried life in service to others. You believe that you are called to some profession or occupation not simply to pass the time, nor to accumulate money, fame, power, or prestige; you know that you are called to find fulfillment and happiness in the service of others. You also know, by faith, that you have an enemy, an enemy of your human nature—Scripture names your enemy as Satan. Jesus, in the words of Scripture we are reflecting on right now, identifies your enemy as "the evil one." He also identifies himself as your protector from the evil one. Believe that. Take courage from the assurance you have of divine protection from the evil one. You are in a lifelong battle with the forces of evil—it would be foolish of you to forget that—but you are not alone in that battle. You have an ally in that battle. You have protection. And you have divine assurance that you will never be tempted beyond your strength. Evil is out there, but evil can be overcome.

Your life is a series of choices; you are making choices all the time. It would be foolish of you to pretend that, in making your choices, you are immune from the forces of evil, that the enemy of your human nature is not at work in this world, trying to divert your will from the will of God. You have to be aware and alert, but you should never be afraid. What then should you do?

First, stay in touch with God—pray to God, listen to God's word, avail yourself of the assistance God offers you through the sacraments of the Church. That's what staying in touch means.

Second, pay attention to your feelings—to your moods and to the interior movements of your soul. What is the source of those feelings? Is the evil one trying to pull you in a direction that is not of God? Is God trying to move you into closer alignment with his divine will? The process of sorting out your feelings and tracing their origin is called "discernment"—discernment of spirits. As I said (and as Jesus says in the Scripture verse we are highlighting today), there are evil spirits at work in the world. You are not immune from the attacks (gentle as they may sometimes be) of the evil spirit.

St. Ignatius of Loyola offers, in his book of the *Spiritual Exercises*, "rules for understanding to some extent the different movements produced in the soul and for recognizing those that are good, to admit them, and those that are bad, to reject them" (*Spiritual Exercises* 313). These are rules for discernment of spirits. What does Ignatius tell you?

In dealing with persons leading a seriously sinful life, the *evil* spirit will "fill their imagination with sensual delights and gratifications, the more readily to keep them in their vices and increase the number of their sins. With such persons, the *good* spirit…will rouse the sting of conscience and fill them with remorse" (*Spiritual Exercises* 314).

In the case of those who…seek to rise in the service of God to greater perfection,…it is characteristic of the *evil* spirit to harass with anxiety, to afflict with sadness, to raise obstacles backed by fallacious reasonings that disturb the soul. Thus he [the evil spirit] seeks to prevent the soul from advancing. It is characteristic of the *good* spirit, however, to give courage and strength, consolations, tears, inspirations, and peace. This he [the good spirit] does by making all easy, by removing all obstacles so that the soul goes forward in doing good. (*Spiritual Exercises* 315)

First, you have to locate yourself (are you on the slippery slope to sin or the upward path to virtue?); then you identify the source (good or evil spirit) of the feeling or mood you are experiencing. If you are on a downward moral slope, the feeling of delight is coming from the evil spirit; a feeling of remorse is from the good spirit. If you are on the moral upside, sadness and anxiety have their source in the evil spirit; a sense of peace is from the good spirit.

Faith tells you that good and evil spirits are at work in the world. The push or pull within you can be from God or not from God. You have to discern the origin of a particular movement or feeling, and in order to do that, you have to give yourself a fair reading of where you stand before God. Are you moving away, on the downward slope—or trying to let yourself be drawn toward God, moving in the right direction? Beware of anxiety and discouragement when you are doing your best to move toward God; they are from the evil spirit! Heed the pangs of conscience when you are on the down side; the good spirit is trying to get through to you.

Let me end with a brief mention of the four preconditions to a successful discernment process, to success in figuring out where God might be calling you to be and do in the world. First, you should be radically free—that is, not locked in to your own way of doing things, not locked in to your own already made-up mind. Second, you have to be radically generous, ready to share yourself and what you have with others, ready to give of what God has so generously given to you. Third, you have to be radically patient—that is, willing to suffer (that's what patience means) if God's will is calling you in that direction. And fourth, you should be united with God in prayer—in touch, and ready to respond.

If you need help in sorting things out, see a spiritual director. If you need reassurance when times are tough, just remember that Jesus was praying for you when he said to the Father, "I do not ask that you take them out of the world but to protect them from the evil one."

31

Vigil of Pentecost

Genesis 11:1–9; Psalm 104; Romans 8:22–27; John 7:37–39

"COME, HOLY SPIRIT, FILL THE HEARTS OF YOUR FAITHFUL"

Who am I to be correcting, amending, or simply clarifying the words you just heard from Sacred Scripture? I'm no one, admittedly, but I do wonder why the Gospel reading can say, as you just heard, "There was, of course, no Spirit as yet, since Jesus had not yet been glorified." The Spirit —the Holy Spirit, the third person of the Blessed Trinity—had no beginning and has no end; the Spirit simply is. The Spirit was surely there as Jesus, the second person of the Blessed Trinity, endured his passion and death and rose again in glory. How, then, can it be said that there was "no Spirit, as yet, since Jesus had not yet been glorified"?

This can only mean, I would suggest, that the Spirit had not yet been given, had not yet been "handed over" by Jesus to those who believed in him. This is the Vigil of Pentecost, my friends, and Pentecost is the day that marks the gift to us of the Holy Spirit who dwells within us. And so today we can pray with the whole Church: "Come, Holy Spirit, and fill the hearts of your faithful." Fill my heart. Fill your heart. Fill hearts throughout the world. Fill every heart with your presence, your power, your love. Come, Holy Spirit!

And the answer to that prayer, that plea, is the powerful presence of the third person of the Blessed Trinity in us, in our world, in an invisible but unmistakably effective way. The Holy Spirit is the recip-rocal love of God the Father for his Son and the Son for his Father. The Holy Spirit is the Spirit not only of love, but of wisdom, courage, reverence, light, creativity, and joy as well. Just think of the infusion of these realities into our lives, into our world. It has happened and is happening; it is all happening now within us. So why are we so bliss-fully unaware? Why are we sleepwalking through such thrilling reality? Let me suggest that an answer to that question lies in another reality, the fact of materialism, the presence of the virus of materialism in our lives and our world.

No reason to apologize for matter. No reason to pretend that we do not need and have to use material things. That is the human condition. But there is reason to be concerned that an overdependence on, an obsessive concern with, and an undue attachment to the material side of our existence might push out awareness of, and engagement with, the immaterial side of our existence. And it is precisely there—on the immaterial side—that the spiritual realities reside. And chief among these, of course, is the presence of the Holy Spirit.

"Come, Holy Spirit, and fill the hearts of your faithful." Reference to ourselves as "faithful" implies that we are men and women of faith. Faith is an immaterial reality. It cannot be seen (except in its effects); it cannot be tasted or touched. Without faith, however, we cannot live a spiritual life. Recall that it was in baptism that we were inducted into the community of the faithful. Recall that with the waters of baptism came the gift of faith and—and this is an all-important "and"—and with the waters of baptism came the Holy Spirit.

Recall the words the Church uses to conclude the ceremony of infant baptism: "By God's gift, through water and the Holy Spirit, we are reborn to everlasting life. In his goodness, may he continue to pour out his blessing upon all present [and this, of course, included you if you ever were present to witness a baptism], who are his sons and daughters. May he make them always, wherever they may be, faithful members of his holy people. May he send his peace upon all who are gathered here."

This is reality. Something real is happening. Just think of the revo-lutionary potential of what is happening and has happened with the coming of the Holy Spirit. *Revolution* means "a turnaround." What an attitudinal turnaround the reality of the presence of the Holy Spirit should bring about in us and in our world.

So it is up to us to free ourselves from our addiction to material things—that's what materialism is, an addiction—so that we can live freely in and with the Spirit, the Holy Spirit, the Spirit of love, joy, wisdom, courage, reverence and all that is good for us and for our world. This is a Pentecost point of view. This is an answer to our prayer: "Come, Holy Spirit, fill the hearts of your faithful."

32

Pentecost Sunday

Acts 2:1–11; Psalm 104; 1 Corinthians 12:3b–7, 12–13;
John 20:19–23

"THEY WERE ALL FILLED WITH THE HOLY SPIRIT"

Pentecost marks fifty days after Easter, fifty days after Jesus rose from the dead. And, as you heard in today's first reading, taken from the Acts of the Apostles, the close friends and disciples of Jesus "were gathered in one place." They were huddled together. They were probably fearful after all they had been through recently. They were surely uncertain and insecure. They were thinking about what was next for them. They were wondering where to go, what to do next. You know the feeling. And then, as the Book of Acts relates it, "Suddenly, from up in the sky there came a noise like a strong driving wind." You know what that sounds like; you even know how a strong driving wind feels on your face and hands.

That wind may have added to their confusion. But notice, they were indoors; the wind must have subsided and it gave way to "tongues as of fire"—a flamelike reality that appeared and "came to rest on each of them." And, as the Book of Acts goes on to explain, "All were filled with the Holy Spirit." They began to speak "in foreign tongues and make bold proclamation as the Spirit prompted them."

This is all quite exciting. Let yourself share in that excitement today. What "bold proclamation" might the Spirit be prompting you to make today? Perhaps you are not all that much inclined to proclaim anything boldly or even in a more subdued fashion. And your reserve in this regard may be a function of the fact that many centuries have elapsed since Pentecost first occurred. Or, it might simply point to another fact, namely, that you and I are locked into secular surroundings that have us buying and selling; lending and borrowing; eating and drinking; speaking and listening; learning and loving; walking, working, and sleeping in a world we regard as self-sufficient and which regards itself as having no need for the energizing presence of the Holy Spirit. That is what might be called a secular outlook—a this-worldly, this-time point of view. Pentecost can change that point of view, if you permit yourself to experience it, to savor it in your imagination.

Pentecost can and should point you to the activating, energizing presence of the Holy Spirit in your life right now and in your world. You can let it happen within you simply by believing. And the basis for your belief is what is preserved for you here in Sacred Scripture and what you have been celebrating liturgically in this season of Easter and Pentecost.

The fact that you commemorate and celebrate today, this Pentecost Sunday, is the presence of the Holy Spirit in your midst in your world today. Secularism blindfolds you to that reality. Worse, secularism deprives you of the peace, purpose, and direction that God intends you to have in your life here on earth. God wants to be the wind at your back. God wants to be the light hovering over you to show you the way.

Similarly deprived are countless people with whom you share space and time on this earth. Secularism is their enemy too. Unwittingly and unreflectively, they are permitting themselves to be deprived by the forces of secularism of the light and flame, the direction and purpose, the energy and peace that the Holy Spirit gives to the soul. These gifts are intended for all. They will be seen as gifts if they become more visible in the lives of believers—in you and me. And if they are seen by more people in our time, they will, by God's grace, be accepted by more people in our time. To the extent that they are accepted, they will work like the wind and like tongues of fire to renew the face of the earth.

That's what the Spirit does. That's why we give thanks today for the gift of the Spirit. That's why we make a Pentecost prayer that the person, presence, and transformative power of the Spirit will be more fully with us today.

In closing, let me repeat for you a prayer of the late Pedro Arrupe, superior general of the Jesuit Order, with which he concluded a Congregation of Procurators (a worldwide assembly of representative Jesuits) meeting in Rome, October 5, 1978:

Lord, we need your Spirit, that divine force that has transformed so many human personalities, making them capable of extraordinary deeds and extraordinary lives. Give us that Spirit which, coming from you and going to you, infinite holiness, is a Holy Spirit.... We desire your profound action in our souls, not only that you descend but that you repose in us, and give us the wondrous gifts that you lavish on your elect—wisdom and intelligence, knowledge and fear of God. Give us that Spirit that scrutinizes all, inspires all, teaches all, that will strengthen us to support what we are not able to support. Give us that Spirit that transformed the weak Galilean fishermen into the pillars of your church, into apostles who gave in the holocaust of their lives the supreme testimony of their love for their brothers and sisters.

33

Sunday after Pentecost: Trinity Sunday

Deuteronomy 4:32–34, 39–40; Psalm 33;
Romans 8:14–17; Matthew 28:16–20

THE MOST HOLY TRINITY

Trinity Sunday always falls on the Sunday after Pentecost, just one week after we commemorate and celebrate the gift we have in the person of the Holy Spirit, the third person of the Holy Trinity. Holy Trinity refers to three divine persons in one God. We can identify the three—Father, Son, Holy Spirit. We can name them, but never fully understand them. They constitute a mystery of faith; the mystery, as we say, of the Most Holy Trinity.

To acknowledge that the Trinity is a mystery at the center of our faith is not to say that we know nothing at all about the Trinity. Each of us has sufficient knowledge of what an earthly father is like to have some idea of what God the Father is like. We are also familiar with the notion of son, so we have some idea of what God the Son is like. And we know that spirit is the opposite of matter and that what is spiritual is immaterial and, hence, not visible or measureable, but knowable nonetheless, just as love is knowable and courage is knowable, as all spiritual realities are knowable, in their effects.

Don't let yourself be put off by the word *mystery*. Instead, let it intrigue you, let it serve to invite you to reflect on the nature of God, and let that reflection produce a sense of awe within you in the presence of the mysterious, all-present, all-knowing, omni-competent, all-powerful and altogether other reality before you in your triune God. That God is your Creator, Redeemer, and Sanctifier. That God is the source of your being. That God sustains you in existence. That God knows you and loves you beyond imagining. And, perhaps best of all, that God is your friend.

You have a friend in the blessed Trinity. You are never alone. You are never without help. You are never without love. You can choose, if you wish, not to think of these things or, worse, you can choose not be grateful for these three persons in your life. But they remain present in you and in your world. They are there and always will be and you are free to ignore them. You are also free to worship them, to give them praise and honor. You are free to give yourself to them—they who are in no need of your love but who invite it nonetheless and who, in receiving it, enlarge your capacity to receive more of their love.

These reflections can lift you to lofty altitudes of thought today, Trinity Sunday, and you should not be afraid to let that happen. All too often we permit ourselves to be trapped in the humdrum, horizonless existence of daily life and foolishly neglect the realization that a personal triune God is alive within us and active in our world. God, in a manner of speaking, is happening all around you all the time.

Trinity Sunday provides you with a special opportunity to deepen your appreciation of this fact. It is a fact of faith, true, but no less a fact because it is made available to you in faith. Savor it today. Be grateful for it today. And continue to live this day gratefully in the name of the Father, and of the Son, and of the Holy Spirit.

34

Sunday after Trinity Sunday: Feast of Corpus Christi

Exodus 24:3–8; Psalm 116; Hebrews 9:11–15; Mark 14:12–16, 22–26

"HE TOOK BREAD, SAID THE BLESSING, BROKE IT AND GAVE IT TO THEM"

Bread broken and passed around. Jesus did that at table with his closest friends. A cup poured out. He did that too. These are signs he gave us; this is a ritual he asked us to repeat "in memory" of him. This is the reality we remember and repeat today on this Feast of Corpus Christi.

"While they were eating, he took bread, said the blessing, broke it, and gave it to them, and said, 'Take it: this is my body.' Then he took a cup, gave thanks, and gave it to them, and they all drank from it. He said to them, 'This is my blood of the covenant, which will be shed for many'" (Mark 14:22–24).

As you hear these words today, I suspect they prompt memories of Masses in which you participated in the past—in the recent past or long ago, some of those Masses simple, some solemn, some in sacred space, others in chapels or cathedrals, some, perhaps, in fields or homes or stadiums. Whether you were young or older, strong or weak, in the company of friends and family, or alone on the edge of the assembly, you were there. And you were there to give thanks, to remember your Lord in the breaking of the bread. You were there to gain nourishment for your soul, to deepen your commitment to discipleship; you were there to hear the word of God; you were there to allow yourself to draw closer to other believers who, like you, treasure the gift of the Holy Eucharist. Corpus Christi—not a city in Texas, but the centerpiece of your Christian life.

"Take this, all of you, and eat of it, for this is my body, which will be given up for you" are words that effect the change of bread into the body of Christ (the Corpus Christi) and at the same time describe the Christian life—the life lived in Christian discipleship—to be lived as bread broken and passed around for the nourishment of others.

The "poured out life" is the expression that comes to my mind when I say or hear the words of consecration spoken over the wine: "This is the chalice of my blood, the blood of the new and eternal covenant, which will be poured out for you and for many for the forgiveness of sins." Just as Jesus poured himself out for us, we are invited to pour ourselves out in selfless service to one another.

These Corpus Christi symbols are powerful reminders of what we are called to be, we Christians, we followers of Christ. They serve to remind us of the revolution of love that Jesus launched at the Last Supper, and that revolution remains to be seen and felt in so many corners of our world. What are we waiting for? Why are we holding back?

The bread of life and the chalice of salvation draw us to the altar. We adore the body and blood of Christ, of course, but we can't permit ourselves to be drawn just for purposes of adoration and devotion.

In the Eucharist, the Church offers us nourishment for the journey of faith. As our "ancestors" ate the manna in the desert and thus had their day's food for their day's march in what was called the exodus, so we moderns have our food for the journey of faith in the eucharistic meal. This is the relevance of Corpus Christi in our day. It is not enough for us, however, to be passive recipients of the Eucharist, we have to get on with the task of discipleship, the task of serving our brothers and sisters in the human community, the task of building a world fit for the arrival of the promised kingdom. That means laying down our lives for one another, loving one another as Christ loved us. It means making the "poured out life" our way of life. It means breaking ourselves out in service as so many loaves of bread broken and passed around, as so many cups poured out.

What are we waiting for?

VI
Ordinary Time

. . . .

35

Second Sunday of the Year

1 Samuel 3:3b–10, 19; Psalm 40;
1 Corinthians 6:13c–15a, 17–20; John 1:35–42

WHERE IS THE PURPOSE IN YOUR LIFE?

There are several themes to bear in mind at this time of the year: the legacy and as-yet unrealized dream of Dr. Martin Luther King; the anniversary of *Roe v. Wade* and the Respect Life rallies occasioned by that anniversary; and the annual Week of Prayer for Christian Unity.

We're not doing so well here in America on all three fronts, when you stop to think about it. Interracial justice is still a distant goal. Respect for life, especially unborn human life, is far from the forefront of our national consciousness. Many Christians are neither praying nor working for Christian unity. There is so much for all of us to do if these goals are to be reached, if these prizes are to be won, if God's will on all three fronts is to be realized.

You have to ask yourself today what you are doing to promote racial justice, to protect life, and to foster Christian unity. I have to ask those questions too. We have to ask ourselves, as the sign on the fence outside the Quaker Meeting House on Florida Avenue in Washington, DC, has been asking passersby: "How Does Your Life Help to Remove the Causes of War?" In a similar vein, ask how your life helps to remove the causes of racial injustice. What difference does your life make in the struggle to protect unborn human life? Ask yourself what contribution you're making to advance Christian unity.

You might find yourself at the movies, as I did once, listening to Jack Nicholson who portrays the recently retired and psychologically depressed Warren Schmidt in the film *About Schmidt*, ask himself: "What in the world is better because of me?"

Let me assure you that there is a lot in this world that is better because of you—each one of you; don't deny yourself the satisfaction of acknowledging that. And there's a lot more that will be better in this world because of you, because of deeds you have not yet done but will do, thoughts that you have not yet had, words that you have not yet said or written. But you will. So put yourselves in a reflective mood today and do some prayerful pondering about purpose in your life. Pray for the discovery of God's will for you.

If St. Ignatius of Loyola could get your ear, as he got the attention of Francis Xavier and other talented and generous searchers for the will of God, if Ignatius could get your attention for a moment or two, he would outline for you his so-called "First Principle and Foundation." It is there at the beginning of his book of the *Spiritual Exercises*. Here is what he would say to you about purpose in your life: "You are created to praise reverence and serve God," Ignatius would tell you, "and by this means," he would say, "you are to save your soul." And "the other things on the face of the earth are created for you to help you in attaining the end for which you are created. Hence you are to make use of them in as far as they help you in the attainment of your end, and you must rid yourself of them in as far as they prove a hindrance for you. Therefore, you must make yourself indifferent to all created things, as far as you are allowed free choice and are not under any prohibition. Consequently, as far as you are concerned, you should not prefer health to sickness, riches to poverty, honor to dishonor, a long life to a short life. The same holds for all other things. Your one desire and choice," Ignatius would tell you, "should be what is more conducive to the end for which you are created" (adapted from *Spiritual Exercises* 23).

That is a formula for a happy life. It is a challenge. It prepares the soil of your soul to accept whatever God wills for you.

The Gospel account you just heard had two disciples, like any two of you, trailing along behind Jesus. As the Gospel story relates it, "Jesus turned and saw them following him and said to them, 'What are you looking for?'" That question turned their lives around. Hear him asking you that same question now: What are you looking for; or what are you looking for in all the twists and turns your life may be taking, at all the decision points you may be confronting: "What are you looking for?"

Go back to the first reading and listen today, as the sleeping Samuel began to listen. He was slumbering, which may be a metaphor for many of us on our occasional sleepwalks through life, but in any case, the Lord called, and Samuel answered, "Here I am."

"The Lord came and revealed his presence," says the Book of Samuel, and the Lord called out, "Samuel, Samuel!" And Samuel said, "Speak, for your servant is listening." Listen he did, and the Lord worked great things through him. Try to bring yourself to a point in prayer today where you can say, "Speak, Lord; speak to me of what you would have me do for peace, for racial justice, for the protection of life, for unity among Christians." "Speak, for your servant is listening."

Who knows where that exchange might lead?

Don't be afraid to ask God what his will for you is. Because with the answer to that question will come not only the disclosure of his will but the grace to follow it.

As pastor of Holy Trinity Parish in Washington, DC, I met one year with the children from grades five through eight, for a prayer service honoring the memory of Dr. Martin Luther King. One of their Scripture readings in that prayer service was from the Book of Exodus (chapter five) where Moses confronts the Egyptian pharaoh to demand the release of the captive Israelites, saying, in the name of the Lord, "Let my people go." I told the children that Martin Luther King had undoubtedly read that story many times and that he heard sung, and sung himself, the words, "Let my people go!" Those words sank into the soul of the young Martin and surfaced to sustain him in his later courageous confrontations with government leaders and law-enforcement officials as the struggle for civil rights unfolded.

When Israel was in Egypt's land,
Let my people go!
Oppressed so hard they could not stand,
Let my people go.
Go down, Moses,
Way down to Egypt's land,

Tell old Pharaoh,
Let my people go!

We've got to be doing what we can to work for the end of oppression and injustice wherever we find it. If we internalize words and phrases from Scripture, those words can work as impulses within us toward justice; they can give us courage, bolster our hesitant spirits.

We are all called to participation in the political process in our representative democracy. Some few of us are elected to responsibilities in government; some are called to other forms of government service. Wherever we are, in government or out, we are Christians called to the promotion of justice, to the protection of life, and the fostering of unity. "What are you looking for?" Jesus asks each one of us as we meet him again today. "They [those two curious early followers] said to him, 'Rabbi'—which translated means Teacher—'where are you staying?' He said to them, 'Come, and you will see.' So they went and saw where Jesus was staying, and they stayed with him that day."

May that be the experience of each one of you today. Stay with him awhile in prayer. Hear him say to you, "What are you looking for?" And ask his help in working out within your heart an answer that matches up with his will for you.

36

Third Sunday of the Year

Jonah 3:1–5, 10; Psalm 25; 1 Corinthians 7:29–31; Mark 1:14–20

ACCORDING TO THE LORD'S BIDDING

Let me invite you to "walk through" our three Scripture readings once again, and, as you do, take an imaginary walk through our city. Let's try to link these readings up with the recent marches we've had here in Washington—marches for life and for peace, and then let us reflect on ourselves, and on the reality within which we live, as we hear the Lord say to us, twenty centuries after he said to a few simple fishermen sitting in their boats mending their nets, "Come after me."

Come follow me, said Jesus, and I will make you fishers of souls, fishers of men and women who are searching for both the meaning and the salvation I have come to give. The search for meaning is part of the human condition. A priest friend of mine used to tell people: "Jesus promises you two things: Your life will have meaning and you will live forever. If you can find a better offer, take it!" That is, in effect, what Jesus said to those first followers: Your life will have meaning; you're going to live forever. That's what he says to everyone who walks this earth.

In the first reading, from the book of the prophet Jonah, you heard that the "word of the Lord came to Jonah, saying: 'Set out for the great city of Nineveh and announce to it the message that I will tell you.'" So Jonah set out for Nineveh "according to the Lord's bidding." And you heard that Nineveh was "an enormously large city; it took three days to go through it," three days to walk across it. The city was known in legend for the enormity of its size and the enormity of its violence and cruelty; its size and its sins were a bit exaggerated in the popular imagination, I'm sure. But the point of the story is to stress the enormity of God's patient forgiveness. The story, as you will recall, relates how the people believed God's word proclaimed to them by Jonah, and because they believed, they repented, and God, because they repented, did not follow through on the threat to destroy them. Hold that picture in your imagination; see Jonah marching across the city calling upon the people to repent.

In the second reading, the selection from the First Letter to the Corinthians, you heard St. Paul say: "I tell you, brothers and sisters, the time is running out." Another alert, another warning. "[T]he world in its present form is passing away," says St. Paul. Indeed it is. Not so swiftly, perhaps, as Paul seemed to believe, but time is marching on; the world as we know it is indeed passing away. The message is clear. Jonah told the people to repent. Paul told the people to be alert, at the ready, not too attached to possessions, not bogged down with the things of this world.

And in the third reading, the selection from the beginning of the Gospel of Mark, Jesus steps into his public life "proclaiming the gospel of God: 'This is the time of fulfillment. The kingdom of God is at hand. Repent, and believe in the gospel.'" There it is again. God's call to preparedness, readiness, repentance.

Why has the kingdom of God remained "at hand," within reach, for these twenty centuries but not yet grasped? Because, I would suggest to you, we have not yet repented, nor have we fully believed his Gospel of justice, love, and peace. God's kingdom is a reign of justice, love, and peace. We have refused to remove from our hearts and from our cities, indeed from our nation and the world, the barriers that our human sinfulness has erected against the coming of the promised kingdom, against the arrival, in our time, of justice, love, and peace. Repent, therefore, and knock down those barriers to the coming kingdom, is the message of Jesus to each one of us today.

Jonah, Scripture tells us, acted "according to the Lord's bidding." What is the Lord bidding you and me to do for peace, for justice, for love, for life? How can we do the Lord's bidding? Were the people who last marched in Washington for peace and life doing the Lord's bidding? What is the Lord's bidding for us? Jonah marched across a major city. Paul addressed the inhabitants of a major city. The march and the message focused on repentance, on conversion, on an attitudinal turn-around, on change. What is the Lord bidding you and me to do today? Should we be marching? What is the word the Lord would have us "hear" before we start walking across our city? What is the word the Lord would have us say aloud, or say only by example, as we walk in this city of ours?

There are often marches in our city for peace and for life. Are your sympathies, if not your feet, with the marchers? Do those demonstrating for peace and for the protection of unborn life raise your hackles or your hopes? Where do you stand on issues of war and peace? And why do you stand where you stand on that issue? Where do you stand on the life issues—abortion, capital punishment, euthanasia, the use of nuclear weapons? Where do you stand and why do you stand there? What is the moral foundation, the moral principle that underlies your stands, your convictions, your choices?

What is the Lord's bidding for us; what is the Lord bidding us to be and to do today in the struggle for justice, peace, and respect for life? Do we need to repent of inaction, of omission; do we need to repent for absence within ourselves of firm moral convictions on these issues?

Each one of us is busy about many things. One way or another, the many things that occupy our attention each day could be compared with the mending of nets that those who fished in ancient days had to do as they sat in their boats. What is Jesus calling us to be and to do today as he calls us to drop our nets and follow him? Hear him say to you, as he said to Simon and Andrew, "Come after me, and I will make you fishers of others, of the men and women, and children who walk through life with you, who walk across this city with you, who march for life, or who choose to march for the choice to terminate unborn life, who march for peace, or for a decision to attack a distant nation." Jesus wants you to walk with him, and work with him for peace, for life, for justice in whatever way you feel called to act.

If you can't march, you can certainly pray. If you don't know where you stand on these issues, you must pray for light. You should also study and discuss and decide, respecting all the while the views of those with whom you may disagree. You cannot just do nothing and let the parade of life pass you by.

Get going with Jonah and wonder aloud whether in "forty days more" our city or any of us "shall be destroyed." Echo St. Paul and tell your brothers and sisters, as well as yourself, that "the time is running out." Get going with Jonah, with Paul, and with Jesus, who is reminding you once again that his kingdom has been at hand for two whole centuries and not yet grasped. It has not yet been grasped because the predisposing belief is not there, and the prerequisite repentance has not yet occurred. "Repent, and believe the Gospel," he is saying to you and me. And we have the very practical problem now of trying to figure out what that means for you and me at this point in our lives, at this point in our journey of faith that began with his call, "Come after me."

37

Fourth Sunday of the Year

Deuteronomy 18:15–20; Psalm 95;
1 Corinthians 7:32–35; Mark 1:21–28

"HE GIVES ORDERS TO UNCLEAN SPIRITS AND THEY OBEY HIM"

There is a lot of strength, reassurance, and comfort to be drawn from careful reflection on this Gospel story. Jesus is asserting here a special authority. And the Scripture says that the people are "spellbound" by his teaching.

Place yourself along with the others there in the synagogue. You've been there before, not this synagogue in Capernaum, but the one in Nazareth. Remember the synagogue in Nazareth where Jesus was handed the scroll at the beginning of his public life and began to read from the prophet Isaiah? "The Spirit of the Lord is upon me, / because he has anointed me / to bring glad tidings to the poor. / He has sent me to proclaim liberty to captives / and recovery of sight to the blind, / to let the oppressed go free, / and to proclaim a year acceptable to the Lord" (Luke 4:18–19).

You then heard Jesus say as he rolled up the scroll, "Today this scripture passage is fulfilled in your hearing." This was a launch of his public ministry, an announcement of what we have come in modern times to call the social apostolate, a special ministry to the victims of poverty and injustice.

Well, here we are in another synagogue. And Jesus is teaching. But his teaching is suddenly and rudely interrupted by the outburst of a "man with an unclean spirit [who] cried out 'What have you to do with us, Jesus of Nazareth? Have you come to destroy us? I know who you are—the Holy One of God!'" Talk about an oppositional setting, an adversarial relationship. Surely Jesus does not want to be drawn into a violent exchange. But there is no avoiding the confrontation. It is a tense moment.

What is the meaning of an "unclean spirit"? This is diabolical possession. This man was possessed by the power of evil. There are now and were then, our faith teaches us, devils, evil spirits, forces of evil, enemies of our human nature at work in the world. Is this an instance of confrontation between the forces of good and the forces of evil? It seems to be. Are those gathered in the synagogue caught, so to speak, in the crossfire of an attack by Satan on Jesus? It sure looks that way. As a scholar commenting on this passage says, this is not a case of ritual impurity. "[T]he man's behavior was due to an outside force under the direction of Satan." (*The New Jerome Biblical Commentary*, 600).

Jesus, in full view of those gathered in the synagogue, performs an exorcism. He acts directly here; he is confident of his authority. Notice that Jesus heals the man by power of his word alone. The Scripture puts it this way: "Jesus rebuked him and said, 'Quiet! Come out of him!' The unclean spirit convulsed him and with a loud cry came out of him."

This is a tense and ugly exchange; notice the shrieks, the cries. This is a frightening scene. Why does the Church put it in front of you today? Why are we modern, civilized, sanitized believers asked to reflect on the reality of diabolical possession in such a grim portrayal?

First, I think, the Church wants to remind you that forces of evil do exist right now in our world. Our journey of faith in this world takes us through a battleground where we can be caught in a deadly attack. Put simply, Satan is out to get us, we who follow Christ. We know that—theoretically and remotely from catechetical instruction received years ago—but do we really believe it?

The point of bringing it up now in a Sunday Gospel story is to protect you from complacency, to shield you from sleepwalking through situations where you might be hurt. You might be playing with pornography or cutting ethical corners in business, cheating on expense accounts if not your spouse, piling up this world's goods instead of doing good works for the poor and disadvantaged. This Gospel might serve as a wake-up call.

The point is not to frighten you, nor to immobilize or discourage you. You witnessed the power of the Lord's word here in this Gospel story. Jesus simply spoke and the demon was driven out. Jesus is there at your side to protect you when you turn to him, ready to speak out in your defense. You can always count on him. But you would be foolish to walk through life mindless of the fact that there is an enemy out there intent on getting you, just not giving it any thought.

Second, I think this Gospel story comes to you as a Sunday reminder in a quiet, reflective moment, that the Church has a kind of Department of Homeland Security all its own. And you are being served by that "department" right now. By word and sacrament, the Church offers you protection. But you have to listen to the word and reflect on it in your quiet moments and make it your own, if it is to be effective in your regard. By sacrament, particularly the sacraments of reconciliation and the Eucharist, the Church fortifies you, inoculates you, so to speak, against the viruses of evil that move unseen through the world that you inhabit. You simply cannot afford to ignore the presence and the power of these sacraments in your practice of religion.

"His fame spread everywhere throughout the whole region of Galilee," says today's Gospel, speaking of Jesus. From this point on, the Church hopes that you will be more attentive to the lurking dangers of evil spirits in your world.

38

Fifth Sunday of the Year

Job 7:1–4, 6–7; Psalm 147; 1 Corinthians 9:16–19, 22–23;
Mark 1:29–39

"IS NOT MAN'S LIFE ON EARTH A DRUDGERY?"

Listen again to the opening of that first reading, from the Book of Job:
"Job spoke saying: 'Is not man's life on earth a drudgery.…My days are
swifter than a weaver's shuttle; they come to an end without hope.
Remember that my life is like the wind; I shall not see happiness
again.'" Wow; pretty grim!

I could have begun this homily by giving you another peek at the
Gospel reading and pointing out the interesting reference to the fact
that St. Peter, the first pope, had a mother-in-law. They say that behind
every successful man—and surely Peter was a success—there is a surprised mother-in-law. You can think about that later on. I want to take
you back now to the Book of Job.

Some years ago, I conducted a research study that led to a better
understanding of how men and women who lost their jobs midcareer
reacted to that very stressful reality. Several of the discouraged job
seekers I encountered mentioned the Book of Job and compared
themselves with poor old discouraged Job, who said, as you heard a
moment ago, that "man's life on earth is a drudgery." Job also said he
had no hope and would "not see happiness again." Can any of you
relate to that?

Identification with Job is easy for deeply discouraged men and
women. One fellow in my study told me that he used to argue with
God, as Job did; he recalled walking down the street one day, both
jobless and optionless, and saying to God, "You don't think I can take
this, do you? Well, make it tougher!" This man thought of himself, he

said, as "a target for [God's] archery" (16:13) and he took to heart the Lord's words to Job to "brace yourself like a fighter" (38:3; 40:2); this was the stance Job chose to take for his complaints and conversations with God.

The reader of the Book of Job is alerted in the prologue, to the fact that Job's troubles were not of God's doing, but the work of Satan. The religious message of the book is that God's ways are mysterious, the mystery of a God of justice who permits good people to suffer. Job's faith and faithfulness are being tested. As the introduction to this book in the Jerusalem Bible puts it: "In his anguish he reaches out for God; God eludes him, but Job still trusts in [God's] goodness....This is the book's lesson: faith must remain even when understanding fails."

Another man I interviewed for my study said he found himself ten years earlier asking himself, "Does the Book of Job have my name on it?" He was in outplacement for nine months. Without in any way wanting or deserving it, he was also in what he called "the Disaster-of-the-Month Club." He had six months of family and financial problems; an unmarried daughter became pregnant; ten days later his wife's only sister died unexpectedly while awaiting brain surgery on her husband; one month later his father died; in April, "the IRS came after me big time"; and he then discovered that his father, a physician, had been "covering" his mother's Alzheimer's disease that was now evident to all and provisions had to be made for her. "I didn't have any dogs licking my sores, but Job and I had a lot in common!" he said to me.

Let's think for a few moments this morning about discouragement in our lives—young or old, rich or poor, working or unemployed, successful or not in studies or on the job. Everyone has to deal with discouragement. And let's also take a moment to think about hope. Hope is the only way to deal with discouragement.

I really like the poet George Herbert's line: "He who lives in hope, dances without music." Hope provides the background music in your life; hope puts the spring in your step when, as they say, "the going gets tough, the tough get going!" G. K. Chesterton, a great Catholic writer, used to say that the more hopeless things became, the more hopeful men and women must be. "As long as matters are really hopeful," Chesterton once wrote, "hope is a mere flattery or platitude; it is only when everything is hopeless that hope begins to be a strength [a virtue] at all."

All of us, young and old, can relate to this. We all get discouraged. We sometimes lose hope. But listen to Chesterton's views—with which you may agree or not—that hope does not come easily to youth. Do you agree with these words of Chesterton? "Hope is the last gift given to man, and the only gift not given to youth. Youth is preeminently the period in which a man can be lyric, fanatical, poetic; but youth is the period in which a man can be hopeless. The end of every episode is the end of the world. But the power of hoping through everything, the knowledge that the soul survives its adventures, that great inspiration comes to the middle-aged." Perhaps you agree; perhaps you don't.

It is true, isn't it, that teenagers think it is the end of the world when they lose a boyfriend or girlfriend, when they lose a game, or flunk an exam. But that just says teenagers and younger kids have to work on being hopeful. God's grace is there to help you in building up your hope. That's why you're here celebrating the Eucharist. That's why we are all here together. We are a people of hope and our hope is in God, a God who is always there for us.

Don't let yourself get stuck in self-pity; don't let yourself repeat the words of Job: "Job spoke saying: "Is not man's life on earth a drudgery....My days are swifter than a weaver's shuttle; they come to an end without hope. Remember that my life is like the wind; I shall not see happiness again." Of course, you are going to see happiness again. And I'm not talking about the eternal happiness that awaits you; I'm talking about here-and-now happiness because you have a heart filled with hope.

Life can be a drudgery at times. We know that. And we have to be sensitive to and caring for others when they are down and discouraged. I wish I knew who left this written message on the lectern in our parish chapel at Holy Trinity one day. The handwriting suggests that these are the words of a woman, I don't know for sure, but listen to the words this unknown person wrote and notice that she is praying for her mother, who appears to have lost hope:

Lord, I know you hear my prayers. You have heard every single one before I was ever born. I feel so much frustration and helplessness now and sometimes even numb where I can't feel you. I've been blessed to come to know you, but I fear that Mom is losing faith and sight of you because we are being tested so harshly right now. Please show her your existence and renew her faith. I know I can remain strong. We need your help, Lord, divine intervention. Without you, we literally cannot survive. We have no more money left and no visible prospects for jobs for any of us. Please, God, help us. I know you will provide because I have asked in your name. Give us peace. And something to hold onto. You told me that if I prayed, this would all be solved. I am trying to be patient, but it is so hard waiting. I feel as if I will burst.

GOD, WE NEED YOU. ARE YOU LISTENING?

ARE YOU THERE?

I don't want to be angry.

Help. Pray for us.

As I said earlier, Job's faith and faithfulness are being tested. This letter too suggests that faith and faithfulness are being tested in our own day, but the writer's faith is strong. As I mentioned in speaking earlier about Job, "In his anguish he reaches out for God; God eludes him, but Job still trusts in his goodness. . . . This is the book's lesson: faith must remain even when understanding fails." What the mother of the writer of this letter needs is hope, and the faith-filled writer herself needs more hope. What each of us needs at various stages of life, in various trials and crises in our lives, is hope. We have to trust in God's goodness. We have to remember that hope is no real virtue unless things are really hopeless.

So let your hope begin. And remember that hope is a theological virtue. Its direct object is God. Your hope is in God, not in yourself. Your hope *is* the Lord, who will never and can never let you down. God cannot ever be anything but faithful to you.

So let's pray for one another that all of us can become better, stronger people of hope!

39

Sixth Sunday of the Year

Leviticus 13:1–2, 44–46; Psalm 32;
1 Corinthians10:31—11:1; Mark 1:40–45

THE WILLINGNESS OF THE LORD

Today's Gospel story raises an interesting question—the question of the willingness of the Lord to respond to our needs. Somewhere deep inside our doubting selves there is a strange hesitation, a lurking suspicion concerning the willingness of the Lord to respond to our requests, to reach out and meet our needs. This is not self-doubt that I'm referring to; it is a doubt we entertain regarding the willingness of God to care for us. In effect, it is a doubt regarding God's love for us. Today's Gospel invites you to make an act of faith in God's love for you.

Put yourself in the place of the leper you meet in today's Gospel. He is obviously in need. He wants to be cured of his leprosy. He approaches Jesus, with a request, "kneeling down [he] begged him and said: 'If you wish you can make me clean.' Moved with pity, [Jesus] stretched out his hand, touched him, and said to him: I do will it. Be made clean."

"If you want to, you can cure me." "Of course I want to. Be cured." There's a concise summary of this exchange, of this encounter. Repeat it in your mind's eye. See the response of Jesus. Hear the words. Note the immediacy of the response: "Of course, I'm willing to cure you. I want to cure you. I've been waiting for you to ask. Why would you even hesitate?"

Yes, there is a certain hesitation on the part of the person in need, but there is also a certain humility accompanied by the courage to take the initiative in approaching Jesus. If you don't put yourself within his reach, he cannot reach out and touch you. If you don't speak out, he can't hear you.

When you look at your situation only from your side, all you can see is hesitation and doubt compounded, perhaps, by the temptation toward self-denigration and the unfortunate conviction of your own unworthiness as a result of your yielding to that temptation. But look at it from God's side and what do you see? You see in this Gospel story that Jesus was "moved with pity." Meditate for a moment on the divine pity. Realize that pity is preexistent to the request in this story; pity is a precondition on God's side as you approach him. God pities you before you even realize your need for pity. And your need for pity confers upon you a certain worthiness to receive the help you need from God.

"O Lord, I am not worthy," we so often say. Of course, we are not worthy, but our unworthiness is no obstacle to the movement of divine pity in our direction. In a broad swoop of "of-course-I-will-it" pity, the Lord is ready to come to you in any need.

You may be saying to yourself now—and I am fully aware of it at this moment—that God does not always respond visibly, immediately, and forcefully to your call for help. You pray and nothing happens. You ask and hear nothing in reply. Your leprosy gets worse; your need goes unattended. Does that mean God's not there, there is no God? No. Does it mean that God is not listening, that God is inattentive to you and your needs? No. Well, what does it mean? It means that God has a plan for you and your salvation that will work out on God's own timetable. It means that God wants nothing but the best for you and the best is yet to come. It means that an act of faith is required of you—faith in God's existence, faith in God's love for you, faith in the presence of the divine pity ready to be released in your regard according to the will of God.

There is a beautiful prayer in every Mass that the priest recites (silently, according to the rubrics) just before receiving communion. The priest addresses Jesus, who is present there on the altar, and says in the old version before the reform of the Roman Missal: "Lord Jesus Christ, Son of the living God, who, by the will of the Father and the work of the Holy Spirit, through your death brought life to the world…." This prayer goes on to ask that through the reception of the body and blood of Christ, the priest may be freed from his sins and from every evil, kept faithful to the teaching of Jesus, and never permitted to be separated from him.

I want you to savor those words "by the will of the Father and the work of the Holy Spirit." They point to both the "plan" (the will of the Father) and the "engine room" (the work of the Holy Spirit) for the delivery of the gift of your salvation. God's will is present in the world. The Holy Spirit is at work in the world. Your job is to connect, as best you can, your will with the will of the Father. Your challenge is to see with the eye of faith that the Spirit is indeed at work in your world and to pray that the "work of the Spirit" may be made manifest in you and in your corner of the world.

This brings us back to where we began, to the assertion that I made at the beginning of this homily. Today's Gospel, I suggested, invites you to make an act of faith in God's love for you. Even though your leprosy may not yet be cured, even though your declared need may not yet be met, God's love for you is real, and his Holy Spirit is at work in your world on your behalf, he is with you and present to you in ways you simply cannot see. All you can do is believe.

And, by the way, you might consider giving God a word of thanks today for gifts unseen and unnoticed. You might begin by thanking the Lord for responding so spontaneously and generously centuries ago when this poor leper stepped up and asked for help. It is never too late to say thanks. Thank the Lord who gave that help. Ask that same Lord to remember you and, by the will of the Father and the work of the Holy Spirit, to permit you, on God's own mysterious timetable, to participate in a generous share of the divine pity.

40

Seventh Sunday of the Year

Isaiah 43:18–19, 21–22, 24–25; Psalm 41;
2 Corinthians 1:18–22; Mark 2:1–12

"MY SON, YOUR SINS ARE FORGIVEN."

There are several things about this Gospel story that I want you to notice.

First, Jesus has apparently been away for a few days and when he returned to Capernaum word got around that he was home—"it became known that he was at home." Word does get around in small towns! And judging from the fact that a crowd soon gathered around the house where he was staying, word about Jesus must have been quite positive, interesting, filled with stories of remarkable sayings and deeds. He created then, as we would say today, something of a "buzz."

Now this is your friend we're talking about here—a rather young fellow. Mary's boy; the son of Joseph the carpenter. He was well known around Capernaum. And you can say without exaggeration that he is also well known to you. Because you are a Christian and a believer, you can say that he's your friend. So having just heard this Gospel story, see your friend surrounded by so many people that the entranceway is crowded; townspeople can't get through. The Gospel account says that he "preached the word to them," to the people gathered there in and outside the house.

You can imagine what he might have been saying. He could have been repeating themes from the Sermon on the Mount—the Beatitudes, for example. He was surely talking about love of neighbor. He may have been suggesting that sin is out there in the world, that unfriendly forces are setting traps for those who want to obey God's law and hope to do the right thing but have to deal with temptation and anxiety. He was on a mission, as you know, and he rarely missed an opportunity to "deliver the word."

Well you've caught him today at an interesting juncture. He is doing his job of spreading the good news when four fellows draw near carrying their lame friend, a paralytic, on a stretcher. They know that this Jesus is a healer; they hope he will heal their friend. That would be the second point I want to call your attention to in this homily—the value of having good friends in your life and the role of friends in making good things happen. This poor fellow had no chance at all of getting within the reach of healing hand and reassuring voice of Jesus on his own; his friends closed that gap for him. Without them, it would not have happened; he would not have been there to be cured. They were resourceful and determined, these four fellows. Big crowd at the house; no problem. Up to the roof they go. They punch a hole in the roof—a fairly large hole—and then lower the stretcher bearing their paralytic friend through the roof right down to ground level where he finds himself at the feet of Jesus.

Jesus was impressed with their resourcefulness but even more impressed with their faith. That's all it took to get him moving in response to their unspoken request. "Child," says Jesus to the unnamed paralytic [other translations have Jesus say, "Son"], "your sins are forgiven." Dwell there for a moment for two additional points I invite you to ponder. Jesus is in his early thirties, thirty-two probably at this time, and, as at least one translation has it, he calls the paralytic, "My son." Does that strike you as strange? There couldn't have been that many years between them, but nonetheless, Jesus calls this fellow "Son." Not "brother" or "friend," but son. He might be using this vocabulary to establish his authority in this particular situation. I certainly don't know. It just makes me stop, and I invite you to stop with me, to imagine again what he looked like—how commanding his physical presence must have been; how authoritative he looked; how much he had of the appearance of a leader. Just being present, just standing, or sitting, or walking around, Jesus was an imposing figure. So we'll permit him to say, "My son" in this particular situation.

But next, notice that he immediately says, "Your sins are forgiven." What sins? Has he ever seen this paralytic before? How does he know he's a sinner, or does he simply presume—as well he may—that every-one he meets is a sinner? After all, he did declare his mission to be one of coming to save sinners. Even without heavy theological speculation about divine foreknowledge and divine omniscience, you can simply conclude that your friend Jesus knows human nature and understands our sinful state, especially back in those early days just before he went through death and resurrection to save all of us from our sins.

Finally, let me ask you to dwell for the moment on the fact that the scribes were there, the oh-so-proper scribes—observing, judging, crit-icizing. "Now some of the scribes were sitting there asking themselves, 'Why does this man speak that way? He is blaspheming. Who but God alone can forgive sins?'" Well, at least the scribes acknowledged the reality of sin but, as you know, their idea of sin was limited to breaking rules, failing to observe the minutest detail of the law. They were liter-alists, fundamentalists, nitpickers. Jesus knew what they were think-ing—notice his supernatural power at work here—and he says to them, "Why are you thinking such things in your hearts?" Without waiting for their reply, he asks the scribes which, in their opinion, is easier—to say, "your sins are forgiven" or to simply say, "Rise, pick up your mat and walk?" He says directly to the paralytic, in effect: "Stand up and be on your way. You are healed!"

And that crowd whom you saw gathered there. What about them? They witnessed all this and the Gospel story says, "They were all astounded." Let yourself be a bit astounded as you relive this experi-ence with your friend Jesus today. "We have never seen anything like this," said the people. Well, neither have you. Enjoy it. Let this event deepen your faith and raise your hopes. And pray that this divine power, which is still able to work in our world, will be active some-where, somehow in our world today to meet the needs of our fallen human race. It can happen; let's pray that it will.

41

Eighth Sunday of the Year

Hosea 2:16b, 17b, 21–22; Psalm 103;
2 Corinthians 3:1b–6; Mark 2:18–22

"I WILL ESPOUSE YOU IN FIDELITY"

It seems that war is on everyone's mind almost every day—the threat of war, the fear of war, the terrible consequences of war, the war or wars that are going on. The threat of terrorism is on our minds too—defending against terrorism, understanding the root causes of terrorism, eliminating the possibility of terrorism anywhere in the world. Our Scriptures tell us that "perfect love drives out fear" (1 John 4:18), but our feelings sometimes suggest that we may be permitting our fears to drive out love.

We need to listen to the prophetic voice, the voice of God speaking to us today through the prophet Hosea. We need to turn to God. We need to seek, search out, and follow the will of God for each of us individually and for all of us collectively, not only "us" as a nation, but "us" as a worldwide community of persons sharing a common origin—in God—and a common destiny—to be with God forever—and our God, of course, is a God of love.

I will leave it to you to puzzle out the meaning of Jesus' words, communicated to you in the selection you just heard from Mark's Gospel, about the inadvisability of pouring new wine into old wineskins. You are on your own to ponder the implications of Paul's words to the Corinthians that "our qualification comes from God, who has indeed qualified us as ministers of a new covenant, not of letter but of spirit; for the letter brings death, but the Spirit gives life." Think about those words on your own and later on. Turn with me now to the first reading you heard in today's liturgy, the selection from the prophet Hosea.

Prophets, as you know, are not those who predict the future. They've become known as predictors of the future only because their warnings were often not heeded and the foretold punishments did in fact come because the warnings were not heeded. The role of the prophet was to point to present problems, usually serious injustices, and to urge corrective action, which, if not taken, would open the door to dire consequences—to punishments of one sort or another—upon the heedless people who ignored the warnings, who refused to take corrective action.

The prophet Hosea, drawing from his own experience of infidelity within his marriage, presents Yahweh, the Lord, and Israel, the nation, as husband and wife. Hosea was not primarily concerned with the anarchy of Israel's last days—that is, before Israel was led into exile and strangers were settled on their land 700 years or more before the birth of Christ. Hosea saw these events as symptoms of fundamental disorder. Israel had forsaken Yahweh. The people that have turned away from its true God, Yahweh, must suffer punishment. But even so, Yahweh remained faithful to Israel, to the covenant that he made with his spouse, despite his spouse's infidelity.

This is a great love story. God's faithful love (*hesed* is the Hebrew word) is a matter of both mind and heart, especially heart, it is abiding devotion to the covenant partner. Listen again to Hosea: "Thus says the Lord: I will lead her into the desert and speak to her heart." And then the prophet has the Lord speak directly to errant Israel: "I will espouse you to me forever. I will espouse you in right and in justice, in love and in mercy; I will espouse you in fidelity, and you shall know the Lord."

Let us pray today that the Lord will speak to our hearts, to the hearts of our leaders, to the hearts of our enemies, to the hearts of those who constitute the United Nations Security Council, to the hearts of all men and women in every corner of the world. Let us pray that we, every one of us, harden not our hearts.

Let us pray for forgiveness of our infidelities. Let us pray for the triumph of diplomacy over armed force, for the eradication of hatred from every heart.

"I will espouse you in right and in justice, in love and in mercy; I will espouse you in fidelity, and you shall know the Lord."

I pray that moments of national crisis, moments when we find ourselves on the brink of war, will be instead moments of national humility, of genuine meekness, not weakness, but an open-hearted simplicity that makes it possible to hear the voice of God speaking to us. I pray that such times will become moments of renewed and lasting fidelity. All of us are sinners; we know the meaning of infidelity. We know that nations, too, can be unfaithful and we pray that our nation may be espoused in right and justice, in love and mercy, in lasting fidelity to the God in whom we say we put our trust. We have to pray that our nation, unlike ancient Israel, will not be seduced by lesser, even petty gods like weaponry and ideology, and abandon its ties to justice, love, and mercy. Justice, love, and mercy could, we know, under conditions of direct attack, prompt us to use our weapons in self-defense. But we are not there at this moment.

Each of us has been forgiven by a God who cannot be anything but faithful to us. We gather every Sunday to celebrate that saving fidelity in the thanks-doing, thanks-saying, thanks-giving that is Eucharist. The God whom we adore is all-powerful—all-powerful. Our God is powerful enough to touch all hearts. Our God can move us to love our enemies, and our enemies to love us. Our God can move us away from injustice toward justice. Our God can take away the impulse toward war and plant within our hearts the courageous conviction to work for peace, mindful, of course, that anyone who really wants peace has to work for justice. And our God is powerful enough to move us to set aside our timidity and speak out and up for peace.

So let us be attentive to the words of the prophet Hosea. And bringing ourselves closer to modern times, let us pray today for ourselves, for the United States, the United Nations, and for our enemies as well, in the words of St. Francis of Assisi:

Lord, make me an instrument of your peace;
Where there is hatred, let me sow love;
Where there is injury, pardon;
Where there is doubt, faith;

Where there is despair, hope;
Where there is darkness, light;
And where there is sadness, joy;
Grant that I may not so much seek to be consoled as to console;
To be understood as to understand,
To be loved as to love;
For it is in giving that we receive,
It is in pardoning that we are pardoned,
And it is in dying that we are born to eternal life.

May there be no dying due to war. May there be a new birth to peace at this hour, a new birth to creative fidelity to the covenant God has made with us, and to justice sealed with love that is the sign of God's covenant with us in our times.

Let's pray that we and our national leaders will have the wisdom to realize that war is now obsolete, that war is no longer a useful instrument for constructive change anywhere in the world. Change is certainly needed in some countries—regime change, a change of heart, a change toward democracy, whatever you want to call it, but war is not the way to bring that change about. Let us pray for the triumph of diplomacy over armed force. Let us remember, as St. Paul reminded the Romans many centuries ago, that "where sin increased, grace overflowed all the more" (Rom 5:20). So let's pray for the release by our all-powerful God of the grace needed to move our world toward peace, especially in the Middle East.

To that end, and toward the end of his pontificate, our Holy Father Pope John Paul II called all Catholics throughout the world to fast and pray for peace, especially peace in the Middle East on Ash Wednesday, the beginning of the Lenten season. We should indeed pray for peace. We should fast for peace recalling, as Catholic tradition reminds you, that there are some evils, some demons, that can be driven out only by prayer and fasting. You know what fasting involves. You know how to pray. John Paul II invited us to be "sentinels of peace" in the places where we live and work; he recommended that we consider praying the Rosary in some quiet place on Ash Wednesday, for peace.

So ponder what Hosea has to say to you today. And consider this one practical follow-up to your prayerful pondering, namely, a day of prayer and fasting for avoidance of war. You may be moved by God's grace to do more, but whatever you do, do not neglect to fast and pray in solidarity with the worldwide Catholic faith community to whom Pope John Paul said in 2003: "Believers, whatever their religion, should proclaim that we will never be able to be happy opposing each other, and that the future of humanity can never be assured by terrorism and the logic of war."

War has lost its logic. Pray now that peace will prevail. God is all-powerful. God can make peace happen if we prepare our hearts, through prayer and fasting, to receive the gift of peace.

42

Ninth Sunday of the Year

Deuteronomy 5:12–15; Psalm 81;
2 Corinthians 4:6–11; Mark 2:23—3:6

"THE SABBATH WAS MADE FOR MAN, NOT MAN FOR THE SABBATH"

There is a solid, guiding principle enunciated by Jesus in today's Gospel, a principle that each of us should ponder and take to heart. Faced with a challenge from the nitpicking Pharisees, Jesus says to all who would be his disciples, to all who would follow him, "The sabbath was made for man, not man for the sabbath."

What might this mean; what is this all about?

Well, you know from the Gospel story that Jesus and his close friends were on the move and it happened to be the Sabbath day of the week, a special day calling for rest and religious observance on the part of God's chosen people according to the Law, the old Law, as repeated in the selection you heard in the first reading from the Book of Deuteronomy.

Jesus and his disciples were moving through a field of standing grain. They did what all of us have done at some time or other in passing by or through a field of grain, or grapes, or growing fruit; they plucked some of the growth for their own consumption. They picked and ate as they walked along. The Pharisees observed this and immediately rendered judgment; indeed the Gospel story says that the Pharisees "protested." "Look! Why do they do a thing not permitted on the sabbath?" And Jesus reminded them that their forbearer, the great David, when he and his men were hungry in similar circumstances— on a Sabbath—did something much more daring. They "went into the house of God . . . and ate the bread of offering that only the priests could lawfully eat." David went into the sanctuary and took the bread and gave it to his hungry men to eat. This happened on a Sabbath. So Jesus said to all of them—the Pharisees and his disciples alike—"The sabbath was made for man, not man for the sabbath. This is why the Son of Man is lord even of the sabbath."

Think of this as a principle to guide your choices and your actions: "The sabbath was made for man, not man for the sabbath." That's a norm, a guideline, a principle that turns the rigid Pharisaic rule on its head. It is an indication of the new era Christ was launching, the era in which we now live, where the spirit of the law, not the letter of the law, would be important; where the freedom associated with life in the Holy Spirit would be the norm for personal choice and action.

This would not be an era of lawlessness. It would not be libertarian immunity from all authority. It would not be a freewheeling, do-what-ever-pleases-you kind of freedom. No, it would be an era of respon-sible freedom. Out from under the thumb of the law or the heel of the authoritarian ruler, the Christian would be an autonomous per-son, a free person, a follower of the Christ whose words (including his commandments and Beatitudes) and actions (including his out-reach to the poor) were intended to set the pattern for responsible Christian living.

It takes a bit of courage to be a Christian, when you pause to think about it. It is easy to substitute authority for thought, to yield personal internal responsibility to external dictates of law and custom and fol-low them just because they are there. You may think that this obedient behavior "gets you off the hook," so to speak, and keeps you on the safe side, but it is really reducing your humanity and shrinking your char-acter. Being a responsible, free, choosing, and deciding Christian is not easy. It presumes formation of conscience as well as character—that's why we consider home, church, and school to be so important in the Christian community. This kind of responsible freedom presup-poses sensitivity to the will of God and generous responsiveness to the demands that the will of God places on each one of us. Sure, human persons—you and I—are a whole lot bigger than the Sabbath, which was made for us in the sense of encouraging our religious practices, and not the other way around; we were not made for the Sabbath. We were not made to be rigid robotic servants of the Sabbath and all the other rules and regulations that once were useful but are no longer needed to foster our growth in union with God. We now live under a supreme law of love. We are capable of thinking for ourselves but we must do that thinking in accordance with the law of love.

It is sometimes difficult to get comfortable in accepting that fact. There is something of the Pharisee in us all. Keep the rulebook handy. Make sure you are in compliance. Be quick to judge those who break the rules. Be slow to notice that some of the rigid rules have long ago yielded ground to the law of love enunciated, by the way, by him who declared himself to be Lord of the Sabbath!

This is not easy territory to negotiate. You need the help of prayer and perhaps you need the assistance of men and women of prayer, spiritual guides—priests, nuns, religious brothers, and reflective laypersons—who are skilled in the ways of the Spirit. They understand how grace works in the soul of the believer. Some people seek this kind of direction in the sacrament of reconciliation, but often that is not the best place, given the constraints of time. Moreover, only priests are there in the sacrament of reconciliation to provide the requested direction. Women—religious and lay—are often skilled in prayer and capable of solid direction. Seek them out. If your parish is not meeting your need in this regard, speak up, let us know.

Similarly, spiritual reading can assist you in your journey. Seek it out. Give it a try. You are still growing; you are developing, regardless of your age. And there's no good reason why you should think you have to go it alone.

I think it would be a healthy thing for all of us to return to today's first reading, the selection from the Book of Deuteronomy, and imagine ourselves to have been bound by that book, so to speak, centuries ago. As you listen think of where you are today.

Take care to keep holy the sabbath day as the Lord, your God, commanded you. Six days you may labor and do all your work; but the seventh day is the sabbath of the Lord, your God. No work may be done then, whether by you, or your son or daughter, or your male or female slave, or your ox, or ass, or any of your beasts, or the alien who lives with you. Your male and female slave should rest as you do. For remember that you too were once slaves in Egypt, and the Lord, your God, brought you from there with his strong hand and outstretched arm. That is why the Lord, your God, has commanded you to observe the sabbath day.

You've come a long, long way, haven't you? And the rules have changed since then. The publication of new directives did not always accompany those changes, but behavior changed nonetheless under the guidance of that "strong hand and outstretched arm" of the Lord. The faith journey continues up to and through this very day. As you continue to make that journey, grow fearlessly comfortable in accepting the truth that you were not made for the Sabbath, but the Sabbath, and all that it represents in the form of custom and practice, was made for you.

Pray to the Lord of the Sabbath for continued guidance and courage along the way.

43

Tenth Sunday of the Year

Genesis 3:9–15; Psalm 130; 2 Corinthians 4:13—5:1; Mark 3:20–35

"WHOEVER DOES THE WILL OF GOD IS MY BROTHER AND SISTER AND MOTHER"

I could title this homily *All in the Family*, but that once-popular television program has long faded from view and memory, and the title might not be all that helpful in gaining your attention. Moreover, there is really no need to try to bring back Archie Bunker!

But it is well worth noting today that the Gospel reading you just heard has Jesus providing you with a ticket of admission right into his family circle. You will recall that when someone shouted out to him that "your mother and your brothers and your sisters are outside asking for you," Jesus replied by asking, "Who are my mother and my brothers?" And he looked around at the crowd surrounding him and continued: "Here are my mother and my brothers. For whoever does the will of God is my brother and sister and mother." Whoever does the will of God . . . think about that for a moment now.

You might find yourself saying that Jesus had no brothers and sisters at home in Nazareth, and you would be right. He had none then, but he has many brothers and sisters now and you could be one of them! Your claim on that title would be based on your honest effort now to align your will with the will of God. Your choices, your goals, your desires, your decisions—to the extent that you do your level best to put them in alignment with what you determine to be God's will for you—are staking your claim to membership in his family, the family that included his mother Mary and his foster father Joseph and Jesus himself, their only son. In this unusual Gospel event, Jesus is opening up membership in his family. You are invited to become a member.

You are welcome. All you have to do is try to discover God's will and follow it.

You have the Ten Commandments. They are familiar to you. They can lead you to the will of God. You have the voice of conscience within you—a familiar voice; it has been there all your life, since late childhood when you began to notice that there were things that you should or should not say and do, simply because your conscience told you that they were the right or wrong things to say or do.

You've had the experience of quiet prayer—reflective moments when you felt the presence of God in your life; moments when you had a sense of divine direction—this way or that, a sense of God calling you one way or another. And that feeling of purpose that you then experienced, that sense of being on the right track, the high road, in your journey through life, that was a feeling of being part of his family. You were relating to Jesus—what greater relative could you have? Having Mary as your mother became possible in this way. Having Joseph as a gentle, fatherly guide was your privilege as well. You were part of a wonderful family.

Perhaps you made some bad choices along the way and cut yourself off from the family. That's happened in other families; it may have happened to you. But the door remains—has always remained—open. You can always return. After all, you're family! They have to take you in.

A few points are made in this same Gospel passage that have relevance to family life. For instance, this text is the origin of that famous dictum that a nation divided against itself cannot stand. "If a kingdom is divided against itself, that kingdom cannot stand." So it is in families—if constant strife is there, the family just won't hold together. But the family that weathers the storms together can emerge from the storms a stronger family.

There is the troubling and difficult-to-interpret passage here about a sin against the Holy Spirit. This is a reference to final despair. "[W]hoever blasphemes against the Holy Spirit will never have forgiveness, but is guilty of an everlasting sin," says Jesus. And the Gospel text explains, "For they had said, 'He [namely, Jesus] has an unclean spirit.'"

The connection here is not at all clear. Surely, Jesus was not possessed by an unclean spirit, although he did have an enemy, a personal enemy Satan, who wanted to possess him and who viewed all those who followed Jesus as enemies as well. Satan would tempt all—including Jesus—to despair. So it seems to me that Jesus is making a plea here to all his followers not to give up on him, Jesus—ever; and not to give up on the Holy Spirit—the Spirit of truth, justice, and holiness—who is the gift of Jesus to those who follow him. Jesus is saying never give up on the power of the Spirit to sustain you, to carry you into eternal life. The giving up would be a form of blasphemy, this text seems to be saying. The giving up would carry one, by one's own choice, beyond the reach of forgiveness. A frightening thought. The insurance we all have against that happening, against giving up, is in our familiarity with Jesus, our being family with him. And we become family by our best effort to align our will with God's will, to live our lives God's way, to let God's values become our values, to make our choices our best efforts to make a reality of the hope expressed in the Lord's Prayer. You know the words so well: "Thy Kingdom come, thy will be done, on earth as it is in heaven."

Well here you are, "on earth," and you can bring his will to earth through your desires and decisions. As a member of the family, this should not be all that difficult for you. Remember, you are a member of the family. Why? Because "whoever does the will of God is my brother and sister and mother."

A beautiful and most reassuring lesson that comes to you directly from the Lord.

44

Eleventh Sunday of the Year

Ezekiel 17:22–24; Psalm 92; 2 Corinthians 5:6–10; Mark 4:26–34

"THIS IS HOW IT IS WITH THE KINGDOM OF GOD"

Let me repeat the opening sentence from today's Gospel reading where Jesus says, "This is how it is with the kingdom of God."

That's something of a promise. In effect, Jesus is saying, "I'm going to explain to you something about the reality of the reign, the kingdom of God." That's what the reign is—a rule, a dominion, what we typically understand by the word *kingdom*. "The reign of God" and "the kingdom of God" are interchangeable phrases. But we've been conditioned to think of *kingdom* in terms of place—palaces, castles, moats, rolling meadows, knights in armor, and so forth. Our images are all so medieval and military. So here we have Jesus saying, "This is how it is with the kingdom of God." And he goes on to speak of seed sown and sprouting up; he speaks of blades becoming ripened wheat, and he speaks of the harvest.

And Jesus goes on to ask, "To what shall we compare the kingdom of God, or what parable can we use for it?" He was a teacher, as you know, and he employed images—often agricultural images—to get a lesson across. Here he is faced with the challenge of teaching his hearers what the kingdom of God, the reign of God, is like. And he uses similes (the reign of God "is like a mustard seed") and he employs parables (a story relating how the small seed eventually becomes a large tree and the birds of the air find in that tree a shady resting place).

There are several things that we can infer from the imagery Jesus chooses to employ here. First, the kingdom of God has a lot to do with growth, and if we can say anything at all about growth, we have to say that it is gradual. So gradual, that although you can surely say you have seen grown grass, you can hardly say that you have watched the grass grow! It is all so gradual.

And you have to go back to that special moment in the ministry of Jesus when he decided to teach us how to pray. You will remember that he told us to pray in these words: "Our Father in heaven, hallowed be your name; your kingdom come, your will be done" (Matt 6:9–10). In other words, he formed a link between obedience to the will of God and the coming of God's kingdom; he presumed here that his hearers would know that there is a relationship between doing God's will and the arrival, the coming, of the reign of God. So we can infer from the teaching of Jesus that, in his view, all of us are like seed planted by him, that all of us need time to grow, and that in our gradual growth we gradually turn toward him—our wills becoming more aligned to his—so that in the alignment of wills—he thought of this as a reign—the kingdom is established. It won't happen without that alignment. And thus aligned—God's will and all human wills—the field that he planted is ready for the arrival of the kingdom. "Thy kingdom come, thy will be done on earth as it is in heaven."

Today's Gospel concludes with the words: "With many such parables he spoke the word to them as they were able to understand it. Without parables he did not speak to them [the general crowd], but to his own disciples he explained everything in private."

Part of that private explanation Jesus gave to his disciples surely had to be a listing of the values, principles, and elements that characterized the reign of God, the kingdom. This has been explained to you countless times through the years. You know that Jesus preached a kingdom of justice, love, and peace. He wasn't preaching a kingdom of power and wealth, of golden streets and mighty fortresses. He had in mind a worldwide alignment of human wills with the divine will. His values of love, justice, and peace were to become the chosen values of those aligned with him in heart and will. The choice, on our part, the choice of love, justice, and peace as a way of life, would be our ticket of admission, title to possession, of the kingdom he came to establish.

It is theologically incorrect—at least inaccurate and imprecise—to speak, as so many of us do, of "building" the kingdom of God. We cannot build it; we can only receive it. "Thy kingdom come," we pray. We do not pray, according to the Lord's instruction, "Let us build the kingdom of God." No. We can and should build the "city of God," which would be a city of love, justice, and peace here on earth. We can (and must) attend to the presence within ourselves of barriers to the coming of the promised kingdom, namely elements of hatred (the opposite of love), injustice (the opposite of justice), and violence (the opposite of peace). So long as those opposing forces are present within us and in our cities, the reign of God cannot come. I like very much the way the official prayer of the Church, the Liturgy of the Hours, puts it in Morning Prayer on Tuesday of the Second Week in Ordinary Time: "Lord Jesus Christ, true light of the world, you guide all humankind to salvation. Give us the courage, strength and grace to build a world of justice and peace, ready for the coming of that kingdom."

We should pray for the courage and strength and grace necessary to do what needs doing, to the extent we can, in order to build a better world—a much better world—of justice and peace that will be ready for the arrival of the promised kingdom.

45

Twelfth Sunday of the Year

Job 38:1, 8–11; Psalm 107; 2 Corinthians 5:14–17; Mark 4:35–41

"EVEN WIND AND SEA OBEY"

Today's readings should have special appeal to those of you who are sailors, who like the sea, who are familiar with choppy waters, both actually and metaphorically, like the ones you encounter in your faith journey through life.

The first reading from the Book of Job has the Lord speaking to Job "out of the storm"; the storm background is used frequently in Old Testament presentations of God. Out of the storm, the Lord speaks to Job and reference is made to the Lord's power to shut the sea "within doors" and to make the clouds a "garment" for the sea, and to employ darkness as "swaddling bands" for the sea. And the Lord speaks to Job of his power to say to the sea, "Thus far shall you come but no farther, and here shall your proud waves be stilled." This is all background reading by way of preparation for the Gospel story. The point to note is the assertion by the Lord of his power over the sea.

And the Responsorial Psalm—Psalm 107—has additional references to the sea. "They who sailed the sea in ships, trading on the deep waters,/these saw the works of the Lord/and his wonders in the abyss." "His command raised up a storm wind/which tossed its waves on high." "They [the waves] mounted up to heaven;/they sank to the depths;/their hearts [the hearts of seafarers] melted away in their plight." More background words and images for the Gospel story: You are in a nautical setting; you are reminded of the power of the waters but also of the greater power of God to subdue the choppy waters. You are reminded of the reality of human fear in the face of storms at sea. You may have experienced something of that fear once or twice yourself.

Then the Gospel of Mark puts you in a boat with Jesus and his disciples. You see Jesus nod off—he is napping there in the boat. You see a "violent squall" come up. You see waves "breaking over the boat" and it begins to ship water badly. Then you see the disciples waking Jesus up and you hear them shouting out to him, "Do you not care that we are perishing?" And you see Jesus sit up, probably stand up, and you hear him say loudly and ever so firmly to the wind and the sea, "Quiet! Be still!" "The wind ceased and there was a great calm."

"Then he asked them, 'Why are you terrified? Do you not yet have faith?'" And there lies the lesson this Gospel story conveys to you today. A great awe overcame the disciples. They kept saying to one another, "Who then is this whom even the wind and sea obey?" A deep calm, an inner peace, should touch you at this moment. You know the answer to their question. You know that it is your Lord and Savior Jesus Christ who can push back the wind and control the sea. You know that Jesus can deliver you safely home through choppy waters, through the trials and tribulations of life. You know that he is there with you in whatever boat happens to be carrying you right now.

From your onshore, safe, and secure observation post right now, you can be forgiven for judging their panic-ridden question during the storm—"Do you not care that we are perishing?"—to be more than a bit ridiculous. Of course it would matter to him, if they were in danger. Of course he would not want them to drown. They were thinking only of themselves, so much so, that they couldn't even imagine that he might be thinking of them too! He wasn't going to let anything bad happen to them.

All this happened on the Sea of Galilee or, as it is sometimes called, Lake Tiberias. Geographically, that body of water is not very large, but it is set below sea level and is subject to sudden temperature inversions and subsequent waves and choppiness. The storm was real. But even more real and much more reliable was the power of God present in the person of Jesus and resident there with them in the boat. That same power is with you today—and everyday of your life.

Your access to that power is your faith. Hear Jesus say to you today,

"Why are you so terrified? Why are you lacking in faith?" Take those questions seriously. Examine your fears. Trace their origins. Consider what needs to be done by you to eliminate them, with the help of God's grace. God wants you to live a fear-free life. Not a reckless or risk-filled life, but a life free of fear of ever being abandoned by or let down by God. God is with you always. You have nothing to fear.

Why are you lacking in faith? Perhaps you take faith too much for granted. Perhaps you pray all too rarely. Perhaps you forget that faith is a gift that you possess and hold within you like a bed of embers, and that those embers have to be fanned now and then with your prayers in order to rise in a flame-like spirituality, nudging you on to good works and to an awareness of God's unfailing love for you.

So climb into that boat today and slip out onto the waters with Jesus. He is there. He may nod off on you, but he will always be present to you. Don't let unfounded fears persuade you otherwise. And never neglect your faith to the point where it ceases to convince you that you are the permanent object of God's undying love and protection, because you are. You can always count on that!

46

Thirteenth Sunday of the Year

Wisdom 1:13–15; 2:23–24; Psalm 30; 2 Corinthians 8:7, 9, 13–15;
Mark 5:21–43

HEALTH CARE AND THE POWER OF FAITH

The longer version of the Gospel reading in today's liturgy contains two striking instances of the power of faith. Jesus is quite explicit in acknowledging one of them when he says to the woman who touched his garment in order to be cured of a chronic hemorrhage, "Daughter, your faith has saved you. Go in peace and be cured of your affliction."

The other instance of the power of faith involves a critically ill little girl. A man named Jairus, a synagogue official, comes to Jesus, falls to his knees before him, and makes an earnest appeal: "My daughter is at the point of death. Please come and lay your hands on her that she may get well and live." The Gospel narrative indicates that Jesus and Jairus walk off together, but then the story is interrupted by the appearance of the woman with the hemorrhage. Immediately after that woman is cured, Jesus, and presumably Jairus with him, are met by people who have come to them from the home of Jairus and they say, in effect, "Too late; the child is dead." "Disregarding the message that was reported, Jesus said [to Jairus]: 'Do not be afraid; just have faith.'" You then have the rest of this very beautiful story where Jesus, together with Jairus and his wife, enter the home, go to the child's bedside, and at the touch of Jesus, the daughter of Jairus comes back to life.

"Do not be afraid; just have faith." These words deserve consideration today. Listen to them, as Jairus listened to them. Ponder them. Take a moment to assess the level of faith and trust in your own life, specifically, your trust in the providence and power of God, your personal God, who knows you by name and is with you in every circumstance of life. Do you believe that God is there for you? Do you trust in his love for you, in his providence and power that are there for you?

Each one of us should insert ourselves into this Gospel story, take it personally, apply it to ourselves. Jesus the healer is in your life today, personally and powerfully by your side, to listen, to help, to heal, to forgive. And he is saying to you that your faith can indeed heal you, that fear is useless, and that what is needed in your life is more trust.

This Gospel reading also provides an occasion to think beyond ourselves, to notice that there is something going on in our broader society—and indeed has been going on for a number of years—that is a public policy issue affecting millions of people and it typically goes by the name of health care reform, I think it should be called health care *finance* reform because it relates to ways we can curb or lower expenditures for health care and how we can extend the coverage of health care insurance to a much broader base, especially to the poor and vulnerable.

Whenever someone mentions health care "reform," I find myself always thinking (and sometimes saying), "No, it's health care finance reform that is the issue," not reform in general. No one wants to dismantle or reform the whole system. It is how we pay for care, how we purchase insurance to cover care, how we lower or control the costs of health care, and how we come up with the money to care for the sick poor that is up for discussion. Money is at the bottom of this public policy debate.

It helps to recall that there are essentially three basic reactions that we humans have to vexing societal problems: fatalism, reform, or revolution. Happily, the nation seems to be waking up and shaking off the immobilizing wraps of fatalism relative to health care reform. We agree that something has to be done. No one appears to be seriously advocating revolutionary change. But, although we talk a lot about reform when we discuss health care, we seem not to realize that reform does not just happen to us; we have to make it happen. And we also tend to avoid precision in defining the problem by omitting the specifics of finance.

There is an accompanying vocational problem that requires attention in the health care debate. We want more talented and generous young people to consider careers in health care. It is distressing to see medical students opt for specialties like cosmetic surgery and dermatology instead of choosing to commit themselves to primary care, internal medicine, and oncology, just to mention a couple of current trends. We need more nurses and nurse practitioners, more physicians, more physical therapists; and we need them there in face-to-face, one-on-one helping relationships with the seriously ill.

We won't get them unless we address the issue of the crushing student loan burden that confronts high-minded young people. Some choose to go into high-paying subspecialties in medicine in order to earn the money that will enable them to pay off their student debt. Why can't that debt be reduced or eliminated in return for a commitment to primary care, and oncological service?

Those who claim we do not need more physicians sometimes say it is a distribution issue, not a question of inadequate supply. They choose to ignore the economic principle that the response to burgeoning supply is lower price, because they recognize that price to the patient is income to the provider. Whoever said health care providers had to be among the highest paid professionals?

There is another window on the vocation issue. The talented and generous young need encouragement to let their deep-down desire to help others be the driver of their decision to dedicate their lives to medicine and nursing and not to make the choice primarily for money or social status. It seems to me that cooperation between Catholic health care and Catholic colleges could help in this regard. Let college students see firsthand and close-up what Catholic health care providers do, especially what they do for the poor.

Two physicians made a startling proposal in a *New York Times* op-ed piece on May 29, 2011: Make medical school free for those who agree to go into primary care. The cost of this would be met by requiring those who choose high-income specialties to pay for their own specialized residency training. Whether that will ever happen I can't say.

Medicare and Medicaid are under attack in the political arena when health care reform is discussed. Their survival will represent a triumph of common sense and regard for the common good. Revenue enhancement (a gentle way of saying "higher taxes") is the inevitable price we'll have to pay. But extending the reach of the healing hand is worth the cost.

Jesus performed healing and curing miracles in response to faith—religious faith in him. As we pause today, in response to this Gospel reading, to check the level of faith and trust within ourselves whenever we present our needs to God, we should also give some thought to the level of honesty and accuracy in the public policy debate about health care. "Do not be afraid, just have faith." Those words of Jesus apply here as well. And as an elderly priest friend of mine used to say, "Jesus is still at work in our midst, but he now works through us, through human hands. That means miracles take a little longer these days, but they can still happen."

It's up to us. Don't let fear hold you back. Don't let trust diminish in your life. And be sure to permit your faith to bring about cures in both your personal life and in the arena of public policy.

47

Fourteenth Sunday of the Year

Ezekiel 2:2–5; Psalm 123; 2 Corinthians 12:7–10; Mark 6:1–6

JESUS TAUGHT IN A WAY THAT MANY WHO HEARD HIM WERE "ASTONISHED"

Today's Responsorial Psalm encouraged you to say repeatedly, "Our eyes are fixed on the Lord, pleading for his mercy." Keep your eyes fixed on the Lord. Plead for his mercy, of course, but notice, as the Gospel story points out, that although he was able to "astonish" his hearers by his teaching, he was a simple carpenter. Keep your eyes fixed on the carpenter.

And you might ask, as you look upon the carpenter Christ, whether you notice the carpenters around you today, whether you see and respect the electricians and plumbers, the bricklayers, seamstresses, and all those who work with their hands. We can easily become elitist without realizing it. We can find ourselves respecting the experts and ignoring, or just taking for granted, the workaday men and women around us who build and maintain our surroundings and keep things moving every day. They all have something to say. Some of them will "astonish" you with their wisdom. But you must first notice them and then listen.

Today's Gospel brings you to another Sabbath and into the synagogue where Jesus manages to amaze the people by what he has to say. The Gospel does not indicate specifically what he had to say; it just goes on to remark that "mighty deeds are wrought by his hands" and reports that the people wondered how a simple carpenter, an ordinary neighbor well known to them all, could pull this off. Unwittingly, they are setting Jesus up to make a statement that has been repeated countless times down through the centuries, namely, that a prophet is "without honor" in his home country. When you are overlooked and under-appreciated, you might find yourself taking comfort from those words, but that is not the point today. The point is that your Lord and Savior Jesus Christ was a person much like you, a working person, whose sense of purpose, whose sense of being sent by a Father in whom he placed his trust, enabled him to say and do truly amazing things. He and the Father were one and the Father chose to speak and work through him.

To a certain extent, the same can be said of you. You can, by faith, unite yourself with God. God can, in his own mysterious providence, choose to speak and work through you. "But I'm only a _____ [fill in the blank]," you might say. Right, and he was only a carpenter. So what else is new? Why are you hesitating?

Notice that the Gospel story states that "he was not able to perform any mighty deeds there" because their lack of faith distressed him. If you are a faith-filled person, you not only raise the level of faith in the place where you happen to be, but you can help to enhance the level of faith in others. Let yourself be transformed by faith and you can assist in the transformation of others.

In selecting the readings for today's liturgy, the Church provides contextual material that is helpful if you are to know and appreciate the powerful person of the carpenter you are meeting once again today. The first reading from Ezekiel reminds you that the Holy Spirit can indeed come to you: "[T]he spirit entered into me and set me on my feet," says Ezekiel; "and I heard the one who was speaking say to me: Son of man I am sending you to the Israelites." Ask yourself to whom are you being sent? You won't know unless you try in prayer to be in touch with the Spirit. And Ezekiel is told that he is being sent to an obstinate, hard-hearted people who might reject him. And that really doesn't matter, this reading says, because "they shall know that a prophet has been among them." You, in your carpenter-like simplicity, may not make much of an impression. Not to worry; they will know that you have been there.

And take another look at the reading from 2 Corinthians. This is a famous and powerful text. If Paul could speak this way of himself, surely you can make his words your own. In order that I "might not become too elated..., a thorn in the flesh [no need to disclose what yours is, just consider honestly what it might be] was given to me, an angel of Satan, to beat me, to keep me from being too elated. Three times I begged the Lord about this,...but he said to me, 'My grace is sufficient for you, for power is made perfect in weakness.' [And so] I will rather boast most gladly of my weaknesses, in order that the power of Christ may dwell with me."

Strength in weakness. Power in helplessness. God's grace will always be enough for you. It worked for the carpenter from Nazareth; it will surely work for you. You can now say most honestly and sincerely with St. Paul, "Therefore I am content with weakness, insults, hardships, persecutions and constraints, for the sake of Christ; for when I am weak, then I am strong."

Savor those words. Ponder them. Make them your daily prayer. There is extraordinary wisdom there just waiting to be understood and accepted by you. Those words can be truly transformative in your life. Words like these were preached by Jesus in the synagogue and those who heard them were "astounded" at what they heard.

You heard divinely inspired, truly powerful words in today's readings from Scripture. Don't just leave them behind here in church when you leave. Later today and throughout the week, go to your Sunday missal or to the Bible and take another look at today's readings. Keep in touch with the carpenter and make the presence of the carpenter felt in your own personal sphere of influence. The results may be truly amazing!

48

Fifteenth Sunday of the Year

Amos 7:12–15; Psalm 85; Ephesians 1:3–14; Mark 6:7–13

TRAVELING LIGHT

Today's Gospel story gives you a glimpse of the strategy and style the Lord expected his apostles to adopt. "Jesus summoned the Twelve and began to send them out two by two, and gave them authority over unclean spirits. He instructed them to take nothing for the journey but a walking stick—no food, no sack, no money in their belts." Wow!

His sales force is going to work with nothing but the clothes on their backs and a walking stick in hand. The pillars of the Church he was out to establish began to address that challenge without a coin and without any baggage at all. They were lean and trim, flexible and light. A walking stick was their only equipment signaling the absence of any wagon or animal to carry them from place to place. It was all so primitive and plain, and, presumably, inefficient and slow.

There was an evident but unexpressed trust in the good will of the people being served to carry the project forward. The servants—clergy and hierarchy—would show up; the ones to be served—the people of God—would feed, house, clothe, and otherwise support those who would minister.

This is stripped-down, bare-bones simplicity. It is also the launch of a movement intended to touch every corner of the world, an enterprise that would become a world religion. And look where we are today! We have permitted the movement to harden into a monument. We've let the community expand into a bureaucracy. True, Christianity has spread and Catholic Christianity is the largest religion in the world. But much of the world remains untouched by the Gospel and the institutional Church we have built up around the Gospel and the Eucharist seems at times to impede rather than facilitate the spread of the good news.

There is not much that any one of us can do about this, at least not in the short term. But each of us can, and should, look to the measure of simplicity in his or her own life. Assuming that we possess and understand the main lines of the Gospel message, we should examine the extent to which we have permitted matter to smother spirit, possessions to crowd out ideas, and power over others to substitute for service to others in our personal lives and in the life of our church.

We can't turn back the calendar and the clock, but we can look back to our roots and try to rediscover the essentials that we seem to have permitted to slip away.

We need a new strategy of simplification in the Church. We need organizational simplification—a modification, but not abandonment of hierarchy. We need architectural simplicity—freedom from encumbering real estate as we focus on the centrality of Eucharist. We need simple and effective communication—from the pulpit in every liturgy and in both electronic and print media outside of liturgical gatherings. But most of all, we need a fresh understanding and renewed commitment to the Eucharist, the central reality upon which our entire religion rests. These four needs will constitute the four points I want to make in this homily today.

Let me begin with the Eucharist.

In the eucharistic liturgy Christ is present to us in four ways: (1) in his word, (2) in his body and blood under the signs of bread and wine, (3) in one another of the faithful as they gather in his name, and (4) in the presence of the priest through whose ministry Christ now offers what he offered on the cross.

Note that Christ is present when the word of God is proclaimed in the assembly—the readings from Scripture and the subsequent homily. And Christ is also present in the assembly of the faithful who are the Body of Christ. Recall that Jesus said wherever two or three are gathered in my name, I'm right there in their midst.

These four modes of Christ's presence in the eucharistic liturgy are, to say the least, insufficiently understood and vastly underappreciated in Catholic worshipping assemblies today.

It takes faith, of course, to see Christ where only bread and wine are visible, but that's what faith does for the believer. It gives sight where vision fails. It will take a lot of faith for people to see Jesus in the person of an unsmiling priest or bishop, even those who try to make themselves more presentable at the altar and less unworthy of their calling to serve the faithful by offering sacrifice.

That sacrifice is also a meal and the people have to attend to their role in gathering around the table not as isolated worshippers but as brothers and sisters in the Lord who recognize Christ in one another as well as in the breaking of the bread.

Architectural simplicity would help if we designed our worship space to bring people together around a table rather than seating them in large theater-like settings where they see the backs of others' heads as they try to focus on distant altars or tabernacles.

Some of those who lead the liturgy today will have walking sticks; they call them crosiers now. But they need not be ornate and there is no need for those who carry them to be overdressed in ornate vestments while carrying titles reflecting royalty rather than shepherd-like simplicity.

Parish rectories and bishops' residences surely need not be palatial. Indeed, it might be time to admit that rectories rarely succeed in serving the dual purpose of providing efficient and accessible office space and private living quarters for the clergy. Might not the clergy be better off living in larger groups of twenty or so in apartment-like structures where they would have a common dining room, enjoy peer companionship, and simply drive to their respective offices and churches each day, remaining always available to parishioners by telephone, e-mail, and other electronic connections?

Compound the problem of aging, if not decaying and overbuilt rectories and churches, with the problem of aging and underutilized parochial school buildings and you have an idea of the strangle hold real estate can get on pastoral ministry that was intended to be an apostolic movement but has hardened into an immobile monument. This is not the case everywhere, of course, but it is reality in a sufficiently wide number of instances in any diocese that it is worth noticing and discussing.

Such discussion will always move toward simplification and, as I said at the beginning, simplification is something we ought to be talking about in the Church today.

49

Sixteenth Sunday of the Year

Jeremiah 23:1–6; Psalm 23; Ephesians 2:13–18; Mark 6:30–34

A DESERTED PLACE

Jesus offers you a bit of good advice in today's Gospel. "Come away by yourselves to a deserted place and rest awhile." Take this as an invitation directly from the Lord. Take it as directed to you. And understand it as an invitation to prayer.

You can pray anywhere, of course. But there are times when you should go apart, separate yourself from the daily routine, seek out some quiet, and listen to the Lord. Speak too, of course, but listen. Quiet down so that you can hear the Lord speak to you.

The place is important. You know from experience what works for you. If you don't know, that probably means that you have not paid much attention to this Gospel-based invitation. To the extent that you have given any thought at all about quiet prayer, you have probably regarded it as something for monks and cloistered religious. You may indeed have noticed advertisements for retreat houses but you probably thought of weekend retreats as something for the overly pious and those with time on their hands, not for fully engaged, overworked persons like yourself.

Let me talk to you today about prayer—especially quiet prayer. There is a wide range of prayer styles with which you are familiar. You participate in liturgical prayer whenever you gather with other believers for the celebration of Mass. You are familiar with private devotional prayers like the Rosary. You may be accustomed to saying your morning prayers and to prayer before retiring at night. Grace before and after meals may be a custom in your household. As a child, you "said your prayers." As a parent, perhaps, you "heard" your children's prayers before tucking them in for the night. Who hasn't prayed before an examination or operation? Who hasn't whispered a quick prayer in moments of danger? And, of course, you don't address your prayer, "To Whom It May Concern." You pray directly to God, the triune God or to one of the three divine persons—Father, Son, or Holy Spirit. You may pray to Mary, the Mother of God, or to a favorite saint, asking them to intercede for you with God.

Now the examples I just recounted involve you praying to God, your words going up, as we say, to heaven. But you should also be mindful that God can speak to you, indeed wants to speak to you, if you would just quiet down and listen! That's why the invitation we are considering today is important—"Come away by yourselves to a deserted place and rest awhile." This is not nap time that the Lord is recommending; this is reflection time, listening time, prayer time.

And it is important that you take time like this to pray, to listen, to enable your will to become better aligned with God's will for you, to tune in, so to speak, to the God who holds your destiny in his hands, who knows you, and who wants to communicate with you. The chances of this happening are vastly improved if you quiet down, go apart, slow the pace, and listen. But when you go apart to pray you do not leave others behind. You do not forget the needs of others to focus on your own needs, you certainly do not detach yourself from the real world of which you are very much a part.

We all know that when Jesus taught his followers how to pray, he did not tell them to say, "My Father." Rather, we say, "Our Father" and repeat the famous words that make up what is known worldwide as "The Lord's Prayer." I want to underscore that point now because you can, if you are not careful, come to prayer with a preoccupation on the "my," the self, and a forgetfulness of the "our" dimension of the approach to God.

"I" have troubles and needs that drive me to pray, but so do "we"—worldwide troubles and needs. To try to go to God without any concern for the needs, joys, fears, hopes, and happiness of others is to display a solipsistic self-centeredness that is unworthy of both the one who prays and the God to whom one lifts his or her mind and heart in prayer. Nothing at all wrong with praying alone, in private and solitude, that is precisely what I'm recommending now; the mistake is to think you can, or should, detach yourself from the rest of the human race in order to be in solitude and alone in prayer. Before God, each one of us is all of us.

There are some presuppositions that apply to any searching, restless, seeking person of faith, who wants consciously to connect with God in prayer. Let me make those presuppositions explicit for you now:

- God is.
- God can be known by faith.
- Faith is a gift.
- The recipient of the gift of faith—the believer—can be nothing but grateful.
- Gratitude is the infrastructure of prayer.
- Prayer—at least the prayer I'm concerned with at the moment—is the flame that rises occasionally and consciously from the bed of embers that is one's faith.

As I've pointed out elsewhere (in the Introduction to my *Book of Quiet Prayer*, Paulist, 2006), the prayer of asking—prayer of petition, as it is often described—is not the sum and substance, beginning and end, be all and end all, of prayer. Not by any means. This is not to say that your prayer of petition is unimportant. It is simply to acknowledge that more advanced forms of prayer, contemplative prayer, for example, and other privileged ways of experiencing God, are available to us poor mortals. Indeed the Holy Spirit wants to pray *within* us, if only we say yes. Nonetheless, the prayer of petition is familiar and just about universal ("Give us this day our daily bread . . . ").

"Gimme, gimme, gimme," is an immature and unsophisticated (even impolite) approach to anyone, let alone to God, your Creator and Lord. Still, God wants to hear from you. Sure, he knows your needs before you articulate them. But in a wonderfully loving and mysterious way, God wants you to enlarge your capacity to receive more and more of his love by stretching out—enlarging—your need-filled soul through your prayers of petition. Ask, and you shall indeed receive.

All too often, however, the prayer of petition is misunderstood and misapplied by the one who makes it.

Reflect for a moment on your own personal experience on a lake, a bay, or river when you are in a boat drawing near to dock. Typically, you would throw a rope (a "line") toward the dock hoping to catch it on a permanent cleat. Once the line is caught on the cleat, you begin to pull. Notice that you are pulling yourself and your boat toward the dock, not the other way around. And yet how often do you toss your prayers of petition up to God, like lines going toward a dock, and immediately try to pull the dock (God) to you! You pray, in effect, for God's will to align itself with yours, for God to come to you, on your terms and conditions, when it should be exactly the other way around.

So, when you pray your prayer of petition—to get that job, make that sale, pass that exam, overcome that cancer—what you must do first is make yourself disposable and disponible to the will of a God who loves you more than you can imagine. Ask for whatever you want, but try to bring yourself to say that you want it only if God wants it for you.

Does God will that you suffer humiliation, pain, suffering? God wills only your ultimate good. God wants to give you love in all circumstances. God may *permit* your suffering, even your victimization, but that is the permissive will (not the direct, positive will) of an all-powerful God at work in the affairs of a world inhabited by human beings whom God gifted with freedom, including the freedom to use their freedom badly—to cheat, harm, maim, murder one another, even innocent others like you. Moreover, you inhabit a world that, due to original sin, the sin of your first parents, Adam and Eve, has an unfriendly environment of illness, disease, and death not originally intended by God for those who love him. The original plan did not include cancer, coronaries, hatred, greed, earthquakes, hurricanes, toothaches, kidney stones, or poison ivy. These harsh realities are part of our wounded world (wounded by sin), a world that in its fallen parts is of our own making, a wounded world that shelters and supports as best it can our fallen human nature. So it makes a lot of sense to pray!

Pray for protection from all harm to yourself and others. Pray for safety. Pray for success, prosperity, good health, long life. But condition your prayers of petition with a "your will, not my will, be done."

What's the use of praying if you can't pull God, your dock, toward you? Because God hears you, wants to give you some things *only on condition that you ask*, and in his own mysterious way prescribes *the exercise of asking* as the means of enlarging your capacity to receive the good things he has in store for you.

You pray to a God of mystery, a personal God, an approachable God, but a mysterious God nonetheless. Therefore, you have to bow your head and trust. God is not altogether unknowable, just not fully knowable, and never fully known this side of heaven. Only God knows God completely.

So be humble. Surely don't act as if you were in fact a know-it-all when you pray. Line yourself up with C. S. Lewis who said it so well: "He whom I bow to only knows to whom I bow." Only God (and those to whom God chooses to reveal himself) knows God. And so you bow. And pray! Jesus is telling you today to go on occasion to some out-of-the-way place and give it a try!

50

Seventeenth Sunday of the Year

2 Kings 4:42–44; Psalm 145; Ephesians 4:1–6; John 6:1–15

THE LOAVES AND THE FISHES

Today's Gospel story is a familiar one—the multiplication of the loaves and fishes—a miracle performed by Jesus to the amazement of the "large crowd" that was following him. It became a bit fashionable in avant garde liturgies not long ago to suggest that the real miracle was that people in the crowd opened up their sacks and shared the food they were carrying with those who had none. That point is worth noting, but it is really far wide of the mark. We're dealing here with a genuine miracle. Jesus did in fact multiply the couple of fish and several barley loaves that a young boy had with him (no mention is made of the degree of struggle, if any, that it took to get the boy to surrender his supply of food!).

There are several lessons that we moderns can take away with us from a consideration of this famous Gospel story. First, we cannot fail to notice the compassionate regard Jesus had for the needs of the crowd. There were no stores or restaurants around. The people were obviously going to feel the need for food; they would soon be hungry. Their need presented Jesus with an opportunity to demonstrate his power (and thus establish his credentials before this great crowd), and there was an opportunity here for him to meet an evident human need. That's what God is like. That's what Christ, who is God among us, came to do—to meet our needs. It seems obvious, therefore, that we should make our needs known, that we should ask, that we should knock, and the door of his divine largesse will open before us. Point number one, therefore, is that the compassionate, powerful, generosity of God, who knows our needs before we do, is at our beck and call; God is standing by to meet our needs.

Point number two is one that I offer in anticipation of subsequent developments in the ministry of Jesus. Point number two is to suggest that this miracle is a forerunner of the subsequent miracle of the multiplication of his presence in the Eucharist. He will, as you know, later take bread, bless it, break it, and offer it to his followers saying, "This is my body." He will do the same with a cup of wine. And he will instruct his followers to "do this in remembrance of me," as we shall do at this altar in a few moments. The remembrance ritual is the Mass. The multiplication of his presence through the words of consecration now brings the real presence of Jesus to every corner of the world to satisfy the hungry hearts of believers everywhere. Talk about miracles! Reflect for a moment on the growing need for priests to bring this miracle about in our own day.

And the third point that I would raise for your consideration in the context of this multiplication story is the fact that there is an enormous problem in our time that calls for a compassionate response from us, namely, the problem of world hunger. The dimensions of that problem are vast. The causes are complex. But the simple fact underlying that complexity is that millions are malnourished today on our planet, and that countless people are dying for want of food. Toward the end of the Gospel story you just heard, Jesus told his disciples, "Gather the fragments that are left over, so that nothing will be wasted."

You might hear him speaking to you today, warning against waste, and reminding you that you live in a hungry world that is broken by unshared bread. Most of us have no direct experience of chronic hunger. Most of us are not living within easy reach of those who do experience chronic hunger. Virtually all of us are simply ignorant of and out of touch with those in other parts of the world for whom hunger is a daily reality, for whom death at an early age due to hunger is a grim reality.

All of us can exercise our citizenship and urge our national government to meet the responsibilities that any rich and powerful nation has with regard to the hungry poor around the world. Many of us can contribute financially to hunger relief efforts at home and abroad.

Some few of us have the training and talent, and are perhaps being called by God, to devote our talent to the scientific discovery, and the economic and political statesmanship needed to eliminate all together the problem of world hunger. That can happen only if we and others in the world have the political will to make it happen.

We Catholics should see this as a moral obligation. We are our brothers' and sisters' keepers no matter where those brothers and sisters live on this planet, no matter what their ethnicity or skin color happens to be. The fact that they are human bonds them to us and us to them. We simply have to open our eyes and see that members of our human family are hungry. Some are dying. All need our help. It is sinful for us to stand idly by and do nothing.

Fr. Pedro Arrupe, the late and great superior general of the Jesuit order spoke at the Forty-First International Eucharistic Congress in Philadelphia in 1976 and made a suggestion that has gone largely unheeded ever since. He suggested that Catholics might consider reviving the eucharistic fast but in a new form. Instead of fasting from food and drink from midnight before receiving holy communion on any given day, Catholics, Fr. Arrupe suggested, might consider "sharing the bread for life whenever they received the bread of life." That means taking some small concrete step to put food in the mouths of the hungry whenever we receive the bread from heaven, the bread of life.

I fail in this regard. I know you do too. But I'm suggesting today that all of us can consider that challenge as we think of the power of God to meet every human need, of the goodness of God in multiplying his presence worldwide in the Eucharist, and of the challenge God places before us to care for the hungry, to do what we can to eliminate the scourge of hunger from the face of the earth.

51

Eighteenth Sunday of the Year

Exodus 16:2–4, 12–15; Psalm 78;
Ephesians 4:17, 20–24; John 6:24–35

THE DAY'S FOOD FOR THE DAY'S MARCH

Every Sunday you hear a reading from the Hebrew Bible; today it comes from the Book of Exodus. You also hear a reading from one of the four Gospels; today, you have a selection from the Gospel of John. Often the Old Testament reading is offered to provide a context for a better understanding of the Gospel story.

When you heard today the story of the manna in the desert, the account of the miraculous feeding of the Jewish people during their forty-year exile, you probably recalled it as a favorite from the Bible stories you read as a child. There is something appealing and fascinating about the story of the manna. You can almost taste this strange food that the Israelites found outside their tents in the desert after they had complained to their leader Moses about their hunger. "Then the Lord said to Moses, 'I will now rain down bread from heaven for you. Each day the people are to go out and gather their daily portion.'"

It was simply miraculous the way this food appeared like dew in the morning and was no longer there once the people had their nourishment for the day. They also had quail to eat in the evening. Each day was a difficult one. Each day was tiring. But the nourishment was always there. Every morning they ate the manna and they moved on. And this, we are told, was their lot for forty years!

And then you hear from the Gospel of John. The crowds are following Jesus and they have plenty of questions for him. Recall the story you just heard from Exodus as you hear the people say to Jesus, "Our ancestors had manna to eat in the desert, as it is written: 'He gave them bread from heaven to eat.'" And that prompts Jesus to say to them: "it was not Moses who gave the bread from heaven; my Father gives you the true bread from heaven. For the bread of God is that which comes down from heaven and gives life to the world."

And then, applying all this to himself and to what he would eventually do for them by instituting the Eucharist, Jesus says: "I am the bread of life. Whoever comes to me will never hunger; and whoever believes in me will never thirst."

Hear those words as coming directly from Jesus to you today. And understand them in the context of the exile, the exodus, the separation of the people from their homeland. And recognize that just as God gave the manna to the Israelites as their day's food for their day's march, so God now gives you the Eucharist, as your food for the journey of faith through this life on your way to the next. Make it your day's food for your day's march, or think of it as your week's food for your week's march.

You are on your way. You will tire. You will grow discouraged. You will hunger and thirst, but, as you heard in today's Gospel reading, Jesus will satisfy your hunger, and quench your thirst; Jesus is here for you, at this table of the Eucharist, to sustain you on your way.

Don't fall into the trap of thinking that you are fulfilling some vague obligation when you go to Mass on Sunday—that you "have to be here" whether you want to be or not, and will "feel better," if you come to Mass on Sundays. No, you don't think that you are meeting some obligation when you enjoy a good meal. Life is tough. Meals are necessary. The journey is long and far from easy. You need nourishment. You are nourished intellectually and spiritually by God's word on Sunday (we fail you if we who celebrate the liturgy do not do that for you), but you are also nourished in spirit by reception of the body and blood of Christ, regardless of what we less-than-perfect ministers do. The bread and wine you receive in holy communion may not do much for your body, but holy communion does everything for your soul. Don't let yourself go without it.

Try to understand the reality of the Eucharist so that you will quite literally know what you are missing when you choose not to be here on a given Sunday. One dimension of that reality is the dimension symbolized for you in today's first reading—the manna in the desert.

When the circumstances of life rough you up, when your friends go south on you, when you lose your compass and your direction as well—when you feel like a nomad in the desert—you need the manna; you need the Eucharist. Don't let some latent form of adolescent rebellion keep you away on Sundays. Come to the table. Remind yourself today of what you might be missing.

As Jesus put it in another context, "Come to me all you who labor and are burdened, and I will give you rest" (Matt 11:28). He will nourish you too. That's why you never want not to show up!

52

Nineteenth Sunday of the Year

1 Kings 19:4–8; Psalm 34; Ephesians 4:30—5:2; John 6:41–51

"I AM THE BREAD OF LIFE"

I invite you to reflect on today's readings in the light of the decline in recent years in Sunday Mass attendance among Catholics. This means, of course, a voluntary separation from the celebration of the Eucharist which, in turn, means a conscious or unconscious decision not to receive "the Bread of Life" that Jesus speaks of in the Gospel reading you just heard.

Catholics who leave their Church to join other faith communities often select congregations where there is no Eucharist, no holy communion; and I have to wonder why that apparently makes no difference to them. Catholics who simply stay at home quite obviously separate themselves from the Eucharist, and again I have to wonder why they seem not to miss the Eucharist.

Now what I am *not* doing at the moment is preaching to those who are not here; I am rather asking you who *are* here to reflect with me on what we might be doing wrong. Where might we be failing those baptized Catholics—some may be our relatives and friends—who, for a variety of reasons, no longer worship regularly in the Catholic Church? Have we let them down? If they don't care, does that permit us not to care?

Have we failed to catechize our young and remind our adult coreligionists about the nature and meaning of the Eucharist? Have we overstressed the Sunday "obligation" and underemphasized the importance of regular, voluntary participation in a faith community—being there because we want to be?

There is something seriously wrong, it seems to me, if you come to Mass on Sunday simply because you "have to." That vocabulary—"you have to"—expanded a bit to read, "you have to because I said you have to!" may well carry you back to your adolescent years and to Saturday night or Sunday morning arguments with your parents. There is something seriously wrong, I say, if people are in the pews on a given Sunday because they "have to be," and not because they "want to be."

Moving from "have to" to "want to" is one way of defining the catechetical challenge the Church is facing today. That is not an impossible task.

The threat of capital punishment is not, I think, a wise way to begin the conversation. You have to go because it is a mortal sin (death penalty) not to go. That is not the way to open up the conversation. You do God no favor by designating him to be the Great Enforcer, the Top Cop, the Executioner. Better to think of God as the Good Shepherd, the father of the Prodigal Son, the compassionate Creator and Lord of the universe.

Our God is a God of love. God's love created us. God's love redeemed us. We are graced and gifted. All we can be is grateful. Now Jesus himself, and the Church he established as a community—a welcoming collection of friends—for those who believe in him, has given us the Eucharist—the body and blood of Christ—as the centerpiece of our religion.

Let faith enter the conversation here. Faith is knowing without seeing. Faith is certain knowledge without evidence. Faith is trust. Faith is hearing something and accepting it as true on the word of another. We believe—because Jesus said so—that the bread and wine offered in thanksgiving on our altars returns to us as the body and blood of Christ. It is ours to receive—in faith—for our salvation.

Now virtually all of us have been introduced to this reality by the use of small, circular, so-called "hosts" made of unleavened bread. They do not look at all like Jesus; they look like flat, round wafers. Similarly with the wine. Neither bread nor wine look like the body and blood of Christ; they look like bread and wine. They don't speak to us, but they do nourish us. Our senses fail us in the face of the Eucharist, but our faith sustains us. How can we address the dimension of "unbelief" that accompanies some to the communion table? How can we make what we see contribute to an appreciation of what we cannot see?

William V. Dych, SJ, was a friend and classmate of mine. He was a Jesuit theologian who studied under the great German Jesuit theologian Karl Rahner and accompanied Rahner as a translator on lecture tours to the United States after the Second Vatican Council. Bill Dych was a creative theologian who died all too young after a teaching career at Woodstock, Fordham, and Boston College. He was particularly effective in explaining the meaning of faith and the symbolism of the Eucharist. He would take bread in his hands, similar to the bread Jesus took in his hands at the Last Supper, and explain that Jesus was, in the ritual of the breaking of the bread, saying in effect to his apostles: This is how I want you to remember me—as bread broken and passed around for the nourishment of others. And this is how I want you to be—like bread broken and passed around, like so many cups poured out—for others.

That social dimension of the Eucharist is so important. This will appeal to the high-hearted young. And this has certain appeal to older Catholics who, through the reception of holy communion, can come to see that they, like Christ, can become bread broken and passed around in service to others, and that in the reception of the Eucharist, they receive nourishment to be and do just that!

"I am the bread of life," said Jesus to you in today's Gospel. "Your ancestors ate the manna in the desert, but they died; this is the bread that comes down from heaven, so that one may eat it and not die. I am the living bread that came down from heaven; whoever eats this bread will live forever; and the bread that I will give is my flesh for the life of the world."

As a wise priest friend of mine used to remark, "If you can find a better deal than that, take it!"

Surely a good deal. Surely one to make any thoughtful person grateful. And let me end these reflections on that note—a note of gratitude.

Eucharist means thanks-doing, thanks-saying, thanks-giving. We give praise and thanks to God every Sunday and we are obliged to do so. But it is not a precept of the Church that so obliges us; it is our condition of being redeemed by Christ, of being rescued from certain death by his own death and resurrection. Our condition is one of gift-edness; so we are grateful.

And, as some of you may recall, the old American vernacular had an expression for gratitude that brings us to where we want to be today in our struggle to understand and correct the Sunday drift in contemporary American Catholicism. That expression in the old American vernacular is "much obliged." "Much obliged" means "thank you." Our Church has chosen Sunday—the first day of the week—to be a special day of eucharistic thanks-giving, thanks-saying, thanks-doing, just as the old Law set the Sabbath—the seventh day of the week—aside as a day of rest and prayer. The new law, established by Jesus at the Last Supper, commands us to love one another, of course, but to love others as Christ loved us (to the point of laying down our lives for one another). We need strength to do that, strength that only the Eucharist can give.

Sunday Mass is the best possible environment for us to show that we are a grateful people, and to do so joyfully in a ritual of praise and thanksgiving. It is up to us who are here to show this gratitude in prayer, song, and sacrament; it is up to us to be a welcoming community for others who, by God's grace, may come to realize that they are "much obliged" to do the same.

53

Twentieth Sunday of the Year

Proverbs 9:1–6; Psalm 34; Ephesians 5:15–20; John 6:51–58

"WHOEVER EATS THIS BREAD
WILL LIVE FOREVER"

The Responsorial Psalm today invites you to "taste and see the goodness of the Lord." You probably associate that invitation with reception of holy communion, and well you might. In the Eucharist you come into direct contact with the "goodness of the Lord," although what you "taste" there is not all that tasty and what you "see"—what meets the eye—is bread and wine. The body and blood of Christ, which is indeed present there, can only be seen with the eye of faith.

In the Gospel reading today, you heard a powerful reminder of just how important reception of the Eucharist is. It carries with it the promise of eternal life. Jesus said to the crowds then, and says directly to you today, "I am the living bread that came down from heaven; whoever eats this bread will live forever; and the bread that I will give is my flesh for the life of the world."

"For the life of the world." Think about that. Death abounds throughout the world. Death in war, death due to illness, accidental death, violent death at the hands of killers, death by one's own hand. You know the words—*homicide, suicide, fratricide, genocide*, not to mention *natural death* which awaits us all. Death does indeed abound in the world, but Jesus promised that his flesh would be given for the life of the world. He would die so that we might live—not just live for a while, but forever. And he offers himself, under the signs of bread and wine in the Eucharist, as a pledge of our immortality, as a promise that we will live forever.

St. Thomas Aquinas wrote a famous Latin text that found a place in the liturgy for the Feast of Corpus Christi that I want to quote for you now: "*O sacrum convivium* [O sacred banquet], *in quo Christus sumitur* [in which Christ is consumed], *recolitur memoria passionis ejus* [the memory of his passion is recalled] *mens impletur gratia* [the mind is filled with grace] *et futurae gloriae nobis pignus datur* [and a pledge of future glory is given to us]."

Pignus is the Latin word for "pledge." In the Eucharist, Thomas Aquinas was saying, you have a pledge of future glory. He also called the Mass a *convivium*—a banquet, a feast—and that imagery carries with it a suggestion of the joyful environment within which this memorial meal should be celebrated.

Anticipating all of this, Jesus, in his public preaching, declared what you heard in today's Gospel: "Amen, amen I say to you, unless you eat the flesh of the Son of Man and drink his blood, you do not have life within you. Whoever eats my flesh and drinks my blood has eternal life, and I will raise him on the last day."

When I taught at Georgetown University, the director of liturgical music for the campus chapel was Jeremy Young, who also composed liturgical music. One of his compositions, copyrighted in 1987, is titled "We Shall Rise Again." The moving refrain to this hymn has the congregation sing, "We shall rise again on the last day with the faithful, rich and poor. / Coming to the house of Lord Jesus, / We will find an open door there, / We will find an open door."

Sadly, Jeremy's wife died at a very young age. Her wake at Blessed Sacrament Church in Chevy Chase, Maryland, just outside Washington, DC, included a prayer service that concluded with Jeremy kneeling at her pine-box casket, closing the lid, and then walking over to a grand piano to play "We Shall Rise Again." The church was filled with friends who gave full voice to the confident hope that "We will find an open door there, we will find an open door." It was a faith-deepening experience for all who were privileged to be present there.

Jesus concludes his "homily" on the Eucharist, the reading you heard in today's selection from the Fourth Gospel, with these words: "This is the bread that came down from heaven. Unlike your ancestors who ate and still died, whoever eats this bread will live forever." The reference to "ancestors" reminds his hearers of the manna in the desert, the food the Israelites received to sustain them during their exile—their day's food for their day's march, so to speak. And the link to the Eucharist is clear.

The Eucharist is here for you today, to nourish you, to sustain you on your faith journey through this life, in this world, on your way to eternal life in the next world. It is a long and sometimes difficult journey. You will experience fatigue—faith fatigue, perhaps—and you will need nourishment. You simply cannot afford to stay away from the table of the Eucharist. If something is keeping you away, attend to it now. Perhaps the sacrament of reconciliation is necessary. Maybe you want to talk to a priest or someone on our pastoral staff. Open up. Unburden yourself.

It is time now for you to "taste and see the goodness of the Lord." One manifestation of his divine goodness is his availability to you and for you in the Eucharist. As you heard Jesus say in today's Gospel, "Just as the living Father sent me and I have life because of the Father, so also the one who feeds on me will have life because of me."

That's a promise. You can count on it. It will carry you home to heaven.

54

Twenty-First Sunday of the Year

Joshua 24:1–2, 15–18; Psalm 34; Ephesians 5:21–32; John 6:60–69

EQUAL BUT NOT IDENTICAL

I may be taking my life into my hands by deciding to preach on the text you have today from Paul's Letter to the Ephesians. You heard the famous words: "Wives should be subordinate to their husbands." You also heard the verse that went immediately before, namely, "Brothers and sisters [note that the brothers are included]: Be subordinate to one another out of reverence for Christ," so there may be some grounds for working the notions of deference and mutual respect into any discussion we might have about this selection from Ephesians. I'll say a bit more in a moment about the full context within which Paul's teaching was offered and should be received.

First, however, let me relate the possible reaction some might have to Paul's politically incorrect and apparently misogynist point of view, to the opening verse of today's Gospel: "Many of the disciples of Jesus remarked, 'This saying is hard; who can accept it?'"

There is no connection, of course, between the Ephesians text, where we hear that "wives should be subordinate to their husbands" and the reading from the Gospel of John, where we learn that some of the disciples of Jesus were "murmuring" in protest and that some chose to walk with him no longer. The two texts just happen to be juxtaposed here by those who chose the readings for this Twenty-First Sunday in Ordinary time.

But there is no doubt that many contemporary Catholics, both men and women, find Paul's words in Ephesians puzzling, to say the least; some indeed find them offensive. Must wives be subordinate to their husbands always? What kind of subordination did Paul have in mind?

Did he have any appreciation of the notion of equality between men and women?

In Ephesians, Paul goes on to say: "Husbands, love your wives, even as Christ loved his church [No one can argue with that.] and handed himself over for her to sanctify her, cleansing her by the bath of water with the word, that he might present to himself the church in splendor, without spot or wrinkle or any such thing, that she might be holy and without blemish.[Again, no problem.] So also husbands should love their wives as their own bodies [Fine. So how did the idea of subordination enter into all of this?]."

We are stuck, I'm afraid, with the translation we have, so we have to make the most of it. That is not to say we have to deny or reject it. Scholars make the point that Paul, however inelegantly in this instance to our ears, is calling for mutual subordination; he is saying to both husbands and wives, "subordinate yourselves to one another." In fact, it can be argued that Paul is narrowing the range of subordination of women in the society and culture of that time, given the infelicitous translation that we have before us. Paul is saying, be subordinate only to your husband, not to all men, as contemporary social norms required.

I can't settle that definitively for you now. I do, however, want to use this text as an occasion to make a point that I think needs attention in our time. Ours is a day and age where women's rights are defended and celebrated, an age when the equality between men and women is just about universally accepted, at least here in the United States. What we need to consider, however, is that while men and women are equal, they are not identical. We often ignore this distinction.

Let me begin with the construction of a paradigm—a theory, or frame of reference, intended to sharpen your focus on this important issue. It is based on my own personal observation, pastoral experience, and extensive reading over many decades. I have found that in addition to the obvious physical complementarity between the sexes, there is a little-noticed and seldom-reflected-upon *psychological* complementarity. Both men and women at all stages of their lives experience varying degrees of discouragement and loneliness, emotions easily activated by job loss, a condition I researched for a book back in the 1990s.

The male, I found, is more bothered by and sensitive to discourage-ment, while the female tends to be more often beset with loneliness than with a feeling of failure in the transition period that follows job loss. This is not to say women do not feel discouraged at times, or that men do not experience loneliness. They clearly do. I have observed, however, that men tend to be more achievement-oriented and women more relational in their approach to work and life. Again, this is not to say that women have no drive to achieve and men are uninterested in forging relationships.

What I am getting at is this: There appears to be a male propensity toward discouragement and a female propensity toward loneliness. Their psychological vulnerabilities *differ* because their psychological propensities *differ*. They are equal but not identical. Failure to achieve can activate discouragement; a failed relationship can trigger loneli-ness. Whether these propensities are genetically rooted and unalterable is not my question to pursue. I simply remark that, generally speaking, *different* tendencies are there. And it is my experience that an aware-ness of the difference can enable spouses or friends to draw closer to one another by permitting their psychological complementarity to come into play. It works this way.

The male needs encouragement in the face of an abiding (it has been there all along, not just in a moment of career crisis!) sense of inade-quacy, self-doubt, and a propensity toward discouragement. The female needs the presence of another, along with the conversation, consideration, and attention that the other person can bring. This pro-vides her with emotional security—a sense of being connected—in the face of a propensity toward loneliness.

If each is attentive to the deeper psychological need of the other, each will enhance the likelihood of having his or her own psycholog-ical need met. The wife who gives encouragement, praise, and personal reassurance to her discouraged spouse, makes herself a significantly more attractive target for the attentive presence she needs and wants. (This is remarkably consistent with a principle of religious faith—"it is in giving that we receive"—that many of us admire but most of us neglect.) In stressful circumstances, like those surrounding unexpected job loss, criticism and resentment from a wife will repel the husband, deepen his sense of failure, and create a chasm rather than a union between the spouses. Similarly, if the wife is the victim of job loss, insensitivity on the part of the husband will only aggravate the relational failure, the feeling of disconnectedness, and the concomitant loneliness.

In *Toward a New Psychology of Women* (Beacon Press, 1976), Jean Baker Miller writes that a woman's sense of self is "organized around being able to make and then maintain affiliations and relationships" (83). Woman feels the need to connect; *affiliative* is a word that helps to describe her natural tendencies and related vulnerabilities. Obviously, it helps the relationship if the male partner is sensitive to this, particularly when a woman's employment relationship or corporate affiliation is abruptly and involuntarily severed.

A full-page advertisement placed by the UJA (United Jewish Appeal) Federation in the *New York Times* on April 15, 1992, pictured a woman staring out through the words of this printed (and timely) message: "My husband got laid off from work eight months ago. Some days are so terrible. He breaks down and tells me he's afraid he'll never find a job. He's afraid I'll stop loving him. And I tell him that's ridiculous. And then I go into the bedroom and cry because I'm not so sure anymore." At the bottom of the page, potential donors to the UJA Federation are told that they can "make it possible for thousands of people to find training, jobs, and most important, dignity."

Dignity is a central issue. Each partner to the relationship should, in the context of job loss, consider him- or herself to be the protector of the other's dignity. And human dignity, you must always remind yourself, is rooted in who you are, not what you do. There is a great American secular heresy that I would call to your attention, namely, that "what you do is who you are." And the unfortunate corollary to this proposition, the one that causes so much grief, is the tendency on the part of those who find themselves "doing nothing" to conclude all-too-readily that they "are" nothing. No one needs to be driven deeper into that hole by an insensitive spouse.

The paradigm I outlined earlier invites elaboration. Men tend to sell themselves short. They often regard themselves as failures waiting to be discovered. This applies to males at all stages and in all circumstances of life. Those men who are rising toward or holding positions on the many managerial mountaintops in contemporary society disguise, even from themselves, their inner fears that they are doing it all with smoke and mirrors, so to speak, and that sooner or later, probably sooner, they will be "found out," "put down," even "let go." Then what? That's the scary question.

Virtually all displaced executives or sidelined managers want to "run something" again, even if there is no financial necessity to do so. They want to prove themselves. They want to achieve.

This is generally true of men, young or old, in all walks of life. Men and women differ in this regard, certainly in degree, if not in kind. And husbands and wives have to understand this. Even when it is clearly a "no-fault" job loss related to legitimate restructuring, men tend to question in the quiet of their hearts their basic competency.

There is a woman inside every man and a man inside every woman. The influence of the feminine in the man and the masculine in the woman is noticeable now where previously there had not been a trace of one in the culturally conditioned preserve of the other. But there are differences that remain and require respect. The sensitive spouse will want to be ready to deal with those differences.

The important question is how will knowledge of the other's vulnerability be used—as a weapon? Or as a reminder that the male always needs reinforcing encouragement and the female always needs companionship? Men and women hold both a wand and a weapon in their hands. They can, in the case of a husband, give attention to a spouse or withhold it. When given, attention becomes reassuring balm; withheld, it freezes into calculated disregard. The wife can offer her spouse criticism or encouragement; criticism drives him deeper in the hole while encouragement gives him hope.

St. Paul would say, subordinate yourselves—husbands and wives—to one another. I would add: know the vulnerability of the other and do your sensitive and loving best to respond to it. As Paul put it in Ephesians, "Be subordinate to one another out of reverence for Christ."

55

Twenty-Second Sunday of the Year

Deuteronomy 4:1–2, 6–8; Psalm 15; James 1:17–18, 21b–22, 27;
Mark 7:1–8, 14–15, 21–23

"BUT THEIR HEARTS ARE FAR FROM ME"

There are two themes from today's readings that I would invite you to ponder for a few moments with me, dear friends. The first will probe the implications of the phrase that Jesus, in order to denounce the Pharisees and scribes, borrowed from Isaiah: "This people honors me with their lips, but their hearts are far from me."

"Their hearts are far from me." How sad. You never ever want those words to apply to you.

The second theme is taken from the Responsorial Psalm, Psalm 15, with the very encouraging words that constituted your response today to the word of God: "The one who does justice will live in the presence of the Lord."

"Their hearts are far from me." "The one who does justice will live in the presence of the Lord."

What is the message God wants you to hear at this hour? Could it be that doing justice is a bridge to the presence of the Lord? Could it be that God is suggesting to you that doing justice is a way of guaranteeing that your heart will never wander far from God, will never remain distant from the presence of the Lord? Think about that.

What then does doing justice mean?

Broadly speaking, there are two kinds of justice that I would invite you to consider today: Ethical justice (giving to each his or her due; treating equals equally) and biblical justice (fidelity to your relationships—your relationship to God, to those with whom you share life on this planet, especially those closest to you, and to the earth itself, which you have from God as gift and hold in trust for future generations of God's children).

Doing ethical justice is what usually comes to mind when you hear the word *justice*; doing things on the up and up, fair and square, on the level. Notice how we borrow from the building trades to explain what we mean by justice. And, indeed, there is a biblical basis for this building-trades approach to articulating the idea of justice. Recall the prophet Amos but remember that prophets are not those who, as the popular imagination portrays them, predict the future. Old Testament prophets like Amos are those who point to the present injustice and warn that if corrective action is not taken, dire consequences will follow. Since more often than not, appropriate action was not taken and the dire consequences followed, the prophet became known as one who foretold the future (the dire consequences). Not so. The role of the prophet is to be God's voice in denouncing an evil and to call for remedial action, and to be God's finger in pointing to an existing injustice. Listen then to the prophet Amos (7:7–9), not one of today's readings, but worth listening to at any time:

> Then the Lord God showed me this: he was standing by a wall, plummet in hand. The Lord asked me, "What do you see, Amos?" And when I answered,
> "A plummet, " the Lord said:
> See, I will lay the plummet
> In the midst of my people Israel; I will forgive them no longer.
> The high places of Isaac shall be laid waste, And the sanctuaries of Israel made desolate;
> I will attack the house of Jeroboam with the sword.

This is the famous image of the plumb line. You see plumb bobs in little holsters on the hips of surveyors. You see them as surveyors stake out the lines and boundaries of new roads and other construction projects. The "plummet" or, as we call it today, the plumb bob, drops directly down from the surveyor's fingers; it is a pointed, cone-like metal weight that seeks the earth's center. The string from the plumb bob to the fingers holding it creates a vertical line—a plumb line—to be seen in the crosshairs of the surveyor's instrument, the transit.

Israel is going to be measured for its uprightness, its justice, says the Lord, through the voice of Amos. If the nation is not upright, if it is "out of plumb," as builders would say, it will surely collapse. Notice, as I mentioned a moment ago, how we borrow from the vocabulary of the building trades to communicate an idea of justice: "on the level," "fair and square," "up and up," "four square." An unjust society will fall just as surely as will a wall under construction that is not straight, that is "out of plumb."

Another image of justice is the familiar scales of justice, the image of two trays in balance on a scale. You see that image everywhere. And all of this relates, as I indicated, to ethical justice.

Biblical justice is something else again; it deals with fidelity, fidelity to our relationships. And it is biblical justice that the psalmist had in mind when composing the words used today in the Responsorial Psalm: "The one who does justice will live in the presence of the Lord." Sometimes the word "righteousness" is used to communicate the idea of biblical justice, but we moderns don't much like that word. It strikes us as archaic or at least a bit formal and stodgy. When we say "oh so righteous," we are not offering a compliment! So, let's stay for a moment with fidelity. Our just God is a God of fidelity. The just man or woman is a person of fidelity. The just heart is the faithful heart, the heart that aligns itself with the will of God, the heart that looks to God.

"The one who does justice will live in the presence of God." The faithful one, the person of fidelity, will sometimes enjoy a sense of God's presence to him or her, a sense of God's "being with" you right here and now.

Sometimes not; sometimes it is faith alone, not sensible experience, that will convince you that God is at your side. He is; he always will be. He will never let you down. He cannot be anything but faithful and present to you. That's why what Jesus said of the scribes and Pharisees cannot be said of those who do justice, namely, that "their hearts are far from me," far from the Lord who cannot be anything but faithful to all of his creatures and all of his creation.

Dwelling, as we have, on this notion of biblical justice—fidelity to relationships, as I've described it—we may now be in a better position to insert ourselves into the crowd that Jesus addressed after denouncing the scribes and Pharisees. Listen to his words. The Gospel story says, "He summoned the crowd again and said to them, 'Hear me, all of you, and understand. Nothing that enters one from outside can defile that person; but the things that come out from within are what defile. From within people, from their hearts, come evil thoughts, unchastity, theft, murder, adultery, greed, malice, deceit, licentiousness, envy, blasphemy, arrogance, folly. All these evils come from within and they defile.'"

Now, of course, many good things, many great virtues and good acts come from within, from the heart of the just person. The point Jesus wants you to grasp is that tainted food or polluted drink enter you from the outside and they cannot defile the real you. (They might make you terribly sick, but they cannot harm your spirit, your inner person, your heart.) If, however, you've permitted your heart to wander far from God, (and if your heart is filled with evil, you've surely wandered too far), if, in any case, you've permitted your heart to wander, you are putting yourself at risk. If your heart is just indifferent, preoccupied, uninterested, and uncommitted, you might ask, "Can these words of Jesus possibly apply to me?" Listen again to Jesus: "Well did Isaiah prophesy about you hypocrites, as it is written: This people honors me with their lips, But their hearts are far from me; In vain do they worship me; teaching as doctrine human precepts. You disregard God's commandment but cling to human tradition."

The tradition won't do it. The formalism won't do it. Lip service won't do it. The externals won't save you. You've got to have things right—righteousness, justice—within. Your heart has to be in the right place and that place is close to God—concerned, interested, and, if not preoccupied with, at least committed to the things of God.

So take those theme-lines, those words from Sacred Scripture, home with you today, dear friends. Ponder them, mull them over, and ask the Lord to instruct you in his ways.

"This people honors me with their lips, but their hearts are far from me."

"The one who does justice will live in the presence of the Lord."

56

Twenty-Third Sunday of the Year

Isaiah 35:4–7a; Psalm 146;
James 2:1–5; Mark 7:31–37

THE SACRAMENTS AND THE SENSES

Let me invite you all this morning to consider two themes suggested by today's readings. First, think about the sacraments and the senses; and second, I'll ask you to consider God's special love for the poor.

The sacraments and the senses—(I have your spiritual senses in mind, your sensitivity to spiritual realities, your ability to see, hear, walk, and speak of spiritual reality.)

In the first reading, you heard Isaiah speaking to "those whose hearts are frightened" and telling them that the Lord is coming to save them. Isaiah says, "Then will the eyes of the blind be opened, the ears of the deaf be cleared; then will the lame leap like a stag, then the tongue of the mute will sing."

The Responsorial Psalm (146) proclaimed that "the Lord gives sight to the blind."

And in the Gospel reading, Mark says, "And people brought to him a deaf man who had a speech impediment and begged him to lay his hand on him." And then Mark notes that:

He took him off by himself away from the crowd,
He put his finger into the man's ears
And spitting, touched his tongue;
then he looked up to heaven and groaned, and said to him,
"Ephphatha!"—that is—"Be opened!"—
and immediately the man's ears were opened, his speech
impediment was removed, and he spoke plainly.

And you will remember that today's Gospel story ends with the words, "He has done all things well. He makes the deaf hear and the mute speak."

There is lots of hands-on activity here. Lots of sense—sight, hearing, speech. There is lots of tangible, physical, sensible reality before you in these readings. That's the way it is with the sacraments; there is stuff—visible, tangible, tasteable, touchable stuff.

In baptism you have water and two different oils. In confirmation there is the chrism, the touch of the celebrant's hand, and in the old days the "blow" to the cheek. In the sacrament of reconciliation there is the human voice and the hand raised in absolution. The Eucharist, of course, involves bread and wine. In the sacrament of the sick there is touch and the anointing with oil. Matrimony involves the joining of hands, the exchange of promises, and often the exchange of rings to symbolize the promises made. In holy orders or ordination, there is the imposition of hands and anointing with chrism. In all the sacraments, there is physical, tangible, audible reality.

In the sacraments, you meet Christ; it is a physical encounter. And through the sacraments, your spiritual blindness, deafness, lameness, muteness—your spiritual undernourishment—is addressed by Christ himself. Through the sacraments, you can walk, see, hear, speak with a renewed self. And it is the Jesus whom you meet in the sacrament that gives you the renewal.

You, of course, must first present yourself to him to encounter Christ in a given sacrament.

It is just possible that the renewal at work in you through the sacraments can sharpen your vision so that you can see the poor in a new way. Sacramental renewal within you may sharpen up your hearing, make it more acute, so that you can hear the cry of the poor. The sacramental strength that helps you overcome your spiritual lameness may also limber up your helping hand and extend your reach in the direction of the poor.

You heard in the second reading today from the Letter of St. James these inspired words: "Listen, my beloved brothers and sisters. Did not God choose those who are poor in the world to be rich in faith and heirs of the kingdom that he promised to those who love him?" This is one of several biblical passages that speaks of God's preferential love for the poor.

Be sure now to get one important point straight. Be sure to understand this: Just because you happen not to be poor is no reason at all to conclude that you are not the constant object of God's unfailing love. God loves you more than you can possibly imagine. There is, nonetheless, a preferential love for the poor on the part of God and the Church—a preferential love for the poor and vulnerable. God loves the poor preferentially, but not exclusively. Some find this hard to accept, this preferential love for the poor. But think for a moment about this ordinary, everyday experience of preferential love, preferential protection....

Imagine a parent and two children walking on a sidewalk beside a busy street. One child is twelve, the other four. The four-year-old breaks free from the parent's hand and darts out into the street into the path of oncoming traffic. The most natural things in the world for any parent to do would be to leave the twelve-year-old to fend for himor herself on the relatively secure sidewalk and dash out to protect the vulnerable child, to show preferential love for the younger child. Why do we seem to have difficulty in applying this familiar reaction to the situation of care for the poor?

Maybe our difficulty in accepting this truth—this preferential love for the poor—could be an indication of a touch of our own personal blindness, deafness, lameness, and muteness—all problems that require sacramental healing. When you meet Christ there in the sacrament of reconciliation and in the Eucharist, give him a chance to touch your ears to hear the cry of the poor, your eyes to see those in need, your lips to speak up on behalf of the poor and vulnerable. It isn't going to happen all at once. That's why you have to "frequent" the sacraments. (Think especially today about the possibility that more frequent use of the sacrament of reconciliation might be helpful to you.)

And to come at this issue of our insensitivity from another direction, let me tell you a story from the rabbinical tradition. This story has been called, "The Window and the Looking Glass." It is taken from a book about the Hasidim, pious Jews who lived in Polish ghettos at the beginning of the eighteenth century.

A man whose heart was hardened by wealth went to the rabbi Eisig. The rabbi said to him: "Look out the window, and tell me what you see in the street." "I see people walking up and down." Then he gave him a looking glass: "Look in this and tell me what you see." The man replied, "I see myself." "So you don't see the others anymore? Consider that the window and the mirror are both made of glass; but, since the mirror has a coating of silver, you only see yourself in it, while you can see others in the transparent glass of the window. I am very sorry to have to compare you to these two kinds of glass. When you were poor, you saw others and had compassion on them; but, being covered by wealth, you see only yourself. It would be much the best thing for you to scrape off the silver coating so that you could once again see other people." (Cited by Charles Journet, *The Meaning of Grace*, trans. by A. V. Littledale, New York, 1960)

So there you are. Two themes. Two points to ponder. Two lines of reflection in the week ahead. The sacraments and the senses; and preferential love, preferential protection for the poor. Test your senses—your vision and your hearing. And try scraping away a bit of the silver in your life in order to see the poor and others who are within the reach of your helping hand.

57

Twenty-Fourth Sunday of the Year

Isaiah 50:4c–9a; Psalm 116; James 2:14–18; Mark 8:27–35

MAGNANIMITY:
AN ANSWER TO THE RIDDLE OF THE CROSS

The words of Isaiah (50:4c–9a) provide a background, an infrastructure, for today's Gospel story. Isaiah's words are easily recognizable; they are used in Holy Week and applied to the sufferings of Jesus:

> I gave my back to those who beat me,
> My cheeks to those who plucked my beard;
> My face I did not shield
> From buffets and spitting.

And the Gospel story you just heard (Mark 8:27–35) is also quite familiar. It lays out the brutal and altogether mysterious strategy of the way of the cross: "He summoned the crowd with his disciples and said to them, 'whoever wishes to come after me must deny himself, take up his cross, and follow me. For whoever wishes to save his life will lose it, but whoever loses his life for my sake and that of the gospel will save it.'"

Tough words. Think them over. Ponder their implications. It is neither flip nor irreverent to suggest that Jesus is saying what a modern hearer might interpret to mean, "Take up your electric chair and follow me."

You can readily admit how difficult it is to "lose your life" in order to find it, how difficult it is to put yourself second (or third or fourth, or deeper down the line). Acknowledge how difficult it is to "take up your cross," "to deny yourself." And yet your happiness depends on your doing just that. This kernel of Gospel wisdom contains the answer to your quest for meaning in life. Here you have a solution to the riddle of life. The message is indeed very tough, but it comes from the same Jesus who said, "Come to me all you who labor and are burdened, and I will give you rest....For my yoke is easy and my burden light" (Matt 11:28, 30).

And when circumstances put you in the number one position—at the top, or near the top—in a group or organization, how mindful you must be, if you want to be a faithful Christian, of the challenge Jesus lays out in these demanding words of Christian discipleship. Deny yourself. If you want to find your life, lose it.

As I pondered those words earlier this week, I went back to Douglas Freeman's biography of Robert E. Lee. I remembered reading years ago these same words on the very last page of the condensed one-volume version (588 pages!) of Freeman's four-volume work:

Had his life been epitomized in one sentence of the Book he read so often, it would have been in the words, "If any man will come after me, let him deny himself, and take up his cross daily, and follow me." And if one, only one of all the myriad incidents of his stirring life had to be selected to typify his message, as a man, to the young Americans who stood in hushed awe that rainy October morning as their parents wept at the passing of [Lee's funeral procession], who would hesitate in selecting that incident? It occurred in Northern Virginia, probably on his last visit there. A young mother brought her baby to him to be blessed. He took the infant in his arms and looked at it and then at her and slowly said, "Teach him he must deny himself."

Notice that Lee was giving a blessing!

What is the message to young Americans today—God's message, the Gospel message; what might the message of a wise and experienced elder like Robert E. Lee be to the young in America today? Let me turn to another elder, another wise person—in this case a poet—for the answer to that question.

Listen for a moment to the poet Robert Frost, who, decades ago, made an annual appearance on the Sunday morning television news show *Meet the Press*. The interviewer is Lawrence Spivak, and the date of the interview is March 22, 1959, when the oldest of the Baby Boomers were in their early teen years.

Question: Mr. Frost, do you think American civilization has improved or deteriorated during your lifetime?

Mr. Frost: I think it has made its way forward, in a natural way, you know. We are so rich that we are like rich parents who wish they knew how to give their children the hardships that made them so rich.

Question: I wanted to ask you about the young people today. Do you think they are more promising? Are they harder, more alert than those of a generation or two ago? Do you think they are better than their fathers or grandfathers?

Mr. Frost: The fear is they won't be if they are made too comfortable and have their life too easy. We are like a rich father who wishes he knew how to give his son the hardships that made the father such a man. We are in that sort of position. We can't. There seems to be no answer to that.

Question: What has been the most important thing, do you think, to you in your life? Love, justice, learning, truth, faith work; or has it been courage?

Mr. Frost: That is hard to answer. I suppose that the greatest thing of all would be magnanimity.

"Magnanimity." How would you have answered that question? What advice would you give to the young? Note, by the way, that *magnanimity* is a good Ignatian word. Ignatius of Loyola advises those who would undertake the retreat experience known as the *Spiritual Exercises* to enter into it with a spirit of "magnanimity and generosity." And the retreatant will come out of the retreat experience with even more magnanimity of heart.

And, by the way, how would you answer the question today's Gospel story puts on the lips of Jesus: "Who do you say that I am?" In attempting to answer that question, you can't avoid these tough texts—Isaiah and Mark; you just can't ignore suffering, sacrifice, and the cross as you try to give your answer to that probing question.

And turning the searchlight on yourself, how might your life, your everyday life, reflect your acceptance of Lee's blessing, and your commitment to discipleship, to the following of Christ after the pattern that he himself lays out for you in today's Gospel? Try magnanimity.

And take another look at today's second reading for a useful clue, a helpful direction in your search for your own Christian identity as a disciple of Christ:

"What good is it, my brothers and sisters, if someone says he has faith but does not have works? Can that faith save him? If a brother or sister has nothing to wear and has no food for the day, and one of you says to them, 'go in peace, keep warm, and eat well,' but you do not give them the necessities of the body, what good is it? So also faith of itself, if it does not have works, is dead." (Jas 2:14–18)

Faith in God is a gift, a grace. Faith, as an act on your part, is a letting go; it is the act by which you entrust yourself to God. Unlike faith, works need no explanation; works are what you do, your actions, your choices. Take an inventory of your "works" to see how well they reflect or demonstrate your faith. Look for the consistency of what you do with what you say you believe. But don't be frightened. Remember: My yoke is easy; the burden I put on your shoulders is light.

Love, for example, is shown in deeds, or it really isn't love at all. You can say you love God and your neighbor, but what are you doing to show that love? What are you doing to show your love of God, of neighbor, of spouse, family, friends, workplace associates?

Where is the magnanimity in your life? Is there enough there for others, especially the young, to see? If they see it, if they catch your large-hearted and high-hearted love of others, including the poor, if the young see the deeds your love produces, you will have done your part to guarantee that they will be OK. You needn't worry about them. Just worry about yourself and your ability to assimilate the wise words of both Robert Frost and Robert E. Lee, not to mention the wisdom of today's readings from Scripture.

If you think about it for a while, you may come to see that magnanimity is a nice summary of all the demands that the Gospel makes of a man or woman of faith. Magnanimity is so quintessentially Christian!

58

Twenty-Fifth Sunday of the Year

Wisdom 2:12, 17–20; Psalm 54; James 3:16—4:3; Mark 9:30–37

"THE SERVANT OF ALL"

"They came to Capernaum and, once inside the house, he began to ask them, 'What were you arguing about on the way?' But they remained silent. They had been discussing among themselves on the way who was the greatest. Then he sat down, called the Twelve, and said to them, 'If anyone wishes to be first, he shall be the last of all and the servant of all.'"

The servant of all. There is something deep down inside of every one of us—mysterious, sometimes unmanageable—that wants to be first. Not ruthlessly first. Not center stage first. Not always in the spotlight, but nonetheless first—successful, achieving, accomplishing, realizing our potential to the fullest. We want to be first and we know that this desire is fraught with danger. Today's Gospel speaks to anyone who feels that impulse, that desire, to be first, and who is also wise enough to know that the impulse must be managed. And notice that the gospel message does not condemn the desire to be first; it simply suggests how best to handle that impulse.

The lesson today is all about humility. And the poster child of humility in this Gospel story is the child around whom Jesus wraps his arms and places in their midst. More on that in a moment.

"If anyone wishes to be first, he shall be the last of all and the servant of all." To unpack that line of good advice, let me first say a word about "servant leadership."

Next I'll say a word about humility. And then I'll close out this reflection with a word about the symbol Jesus chose to use to represent humility and servant leadership—the child.

First, servant leadership. The expression comes from Robert K. Greenleaf whose book bearing that title—*Servant Leadership*—has the subtitle: *A Journey into the Nature of Legitimate Power and Greatness.* If you, like the earliest disciples of Jesus, want to argue about "who is the greatest," go ahead. That's fine. But argue from the base of an appreciation of the "nature of legitimate power and greatness."

Legitimate power, like power in any circumstance, is the ability to bring about or prevent change. But legitimate, properly constituted power would speak to those concerned with exercising their power appropriately and achieving greatness, properly understood, to be, as Gandhi once said, the change you want to see happen. Be the change you are calling for in your complaints, your dreams, and your prayers. If you want change, be the change you are looking for.

All power is relational. You may mistakenly think of power as something you possess, something you can carry or move around to do your bidding. You may think of power in terms of money; the more you have the more powerful you are. No, power is relational. If the relational empowerment is withdrawn, there is no power. For example, you in this church are empowering me at this moment to preach. If you withdrew your presence, I'd have no one to whom to preach; there would be no homily.

In the opening chapter of *Servant Leadership*, Greenleaf writes of "The Servant as Leader." He might just as well have titled that essay, "The Leader as Servant."

Listen for a moment to Robert Greenleaf: "A fresh critical look is being taken at the issues of power and authority, and people are beginning to learn, however haltingly, to relate to one another in less coercive and more creatively supporting ways. A new moral principle is emerging which holds that the only authority deserving one's allegiance is that which is freely and knowingly granted by the led to the leader in response to, and in proportion to, the clearly evident servant stature of the leader."

Let me note that Robert Greenleaf was not taking as the primary referent political leadership, those who say they aspire to become "servants of the people" and who campaign on servant rhetoric that is too often set aside shortly after the votes are tallied. He was writing out of the experience of institutional turmoil in the 1960s and '70s—institutions large and small, primarily private sector institutions and groups, including families. He was writing out of the conviction that the only truly viable institutions will be those that are servant led.

In effect, Jesus is saying the same thing to you in today's Gospel—wherever you fit into the picture, whatever responsibilities you have in whatever group. Wherever and however you relate to others—in family, business, school, profession, government, or other organization of any kind and any size—wherever and however you relate to others, relate as a servant and you will, indeed, be a leader. You will have discovered the way to become the "greatest." Mahatma Gandhi came to this conclusion from another direction when he said: "There comes a time when an individual becomes irresistible and his action becomes all pervasive in its effect. This comes when he reduces himself to zero."

Servant leadership, as you can see, presupposes a certain level of humility. How do you understand humility? When you think of Jesus as "meek and humble of heart," do pastel portrayals in holy card art deliver to your mind's eye a picture of weakness, rather than true meekness, or timidity, rather than true humility? Humility is a virtue; timidity is a vice. Humility is courage, the spirit of the cross. "The Son of Man is to be handed over to men and they will kill him," Jesus forthrightly and courageously tells his disciples in today's Gospel reading, "And three days after his death the Son of Man will rise," he adds with a note of confidence—confidence in the Father who will indeed raise him from the dead. This is the voice of courage speaking. Each one of you is capable of that kind of faith-based courage. Each one of you is capable of true humility.

What is humility? That, of course, is a hard question to answer. Try answering it for yourself.

For the parent or teacher, humility may be the acceptance of the fact that you are making yourself progressively less necessary. For the successful achiever, it may be the realization of your own complete dependency. St. Augustine saw humility as "the complete acknowledgment of our total dependence on God," and he called that insight "the root of all perfection." For any one of us, humility may be the realization that Christ chooses to build his dwelling within us on the ruins of our own self-love (let the excavation of self begin!). Or, we can acknowledge that as a people we've learned to fly the skies like birds and swim the seas like fish, but we still need to learn how to walk the earth like humans, like sons and daughters of an all-wise Creator. Humility is another word for having a lot to learn.

And there, perhaps, is a clue to the reason why Jesus put a little child before them to make his disciples aware of the meaning of humility. Children, by definition, have a lot to learn. They are open, natural, unaffected, trusting. They are literally and figuratively learning how to walk the earth like humans.

All too often, we adults allow our timidity to assume a fake identity, to wear the colors of humility, when, in fact, cowardice, not courage, is at work within us. Like Hamlet, we know that "conscience doth make cowards of us all." We should be humble enough to admit that, and consoled to know that such an admission is a step forward on the road to humility, to becoming like little children who are naturally shy but innocent, whose consciences can eventually make courageous Christians of them all. Christ invites you to clarity of conscience, to courage, to humility, as he says: "Whoever receives one child such as this in my name, receives me; and whoever receives me, receives not me but the One who sent me."

This is not about childcare, or child protection, or child development; it is all about the care, protection, and development within you of the great virtue of humility. Become humble and you receive Christ. Receive Christ and you receive the One who sent him. That's how you can become "the greatest." That's what will happen if you determine to become "the servant of all."

59

Twenty-Sixth Sunday of the Year

Numbers 11:25–29; Psalm 19; James 5:1–6; Mark 9:38–43, 45, 47–48

THE MILLSTONE

"Whoever causes one of these little ones who believes in me to sin, it would be better for him if a great millstone were put around his neck and he were thrown into the sea" (Mark 9:42).

It would be helpful right here at the outset, to take a moment to make sure we have a clear understanding of scandal, of what it means to cause another to sin—the technical meaning of scandal—and then move on to consider (1) the millstone, (2) the surgical metaphor Jesus is using in this Gospel message, and (3) the applicability of all this to what is happening in our world today.

We use the word *scandal* so often and so loosely, that we tend to forget its technical meaning. Scandal causes another to sin. It is not simply something that raises eyebrows, has a certain shock value, creates confusion, causes disgust. Scandal causes another to sin. You may say you are "scandalized" by inappropriate behavior, but if the "scandalous" activity does not cause you or another to sin, it is not, in fact, scandalous; it is simply repugnant, unworthy, and reprehensible. Scandal, in the strict sense of the word, causes another to sin; it blocks another's path to virtue. That's why Jesus uses millstone language in the instance of someone causing a "little one" to sin.

In the days Jesus walked the earth, the millstone was a common household appliance for grinding flour. But there were also milling houses with heavier stones. Whether at home or in the mill, the stones—rough surfaced and strong; one upper and the other lower—were necessary to reduce grain to meal or flour. Milling was a routine part of domestic and village life. The reference in this Gospel passage is to the heavy upper stone from the rotary mill; the stone that was heavy enough to really get the job done.

If someone causes a child or an immature believer to sin, that behavior merits the millstone. More on that in just a moment.

It is also important to understand that Jesus is not talking about bodily mutilation in this Gospel passage. Consider how often you use the expression, "Cut it out!" "If you don't cut that out right now. . . . " You get a little nervous when you hear that if your hand causes you to sin, if your foot causes you to sin, if your eye causes you to sin, you should immediately resort to radical surgery. Radical? Yes. Surgery? Only in a metaphorical sense. These sayings are really about your attitudes, your dispositions, your inclinations, your readiness for the new way of life Jesus was proclaiming. You have to cut out of your life those practices, places, possessions, persons, and habits that are pulling you away from God. Hold onto habits, practices, places, possessions, and persons only if they help; away with them if they hinder! You know what is required. How often do you apply the surgical remedy to others with the command, "Cut it out!" Apply it now to yourself.

Radical surgery in the spiritual order is what Jesus is talking about. Most of us need to pay close attention to that message. But let's return to the millstone and the person who causes a "little one" to sin.

Early one Monday morning, I was pondering this Scripture passage and trying to figure out what the Lord might want me to say about it in the Sunday homily. Later that same Monday morning, I read the following words on the front page of the *New York Times*:

In their house in Yellow Springs, Ohio, Will Lapedes and his parents were negotiating a conflict over electronic turf. Will, 14, wanted a computer in his room. For his parents, this raised a red flag. "We wanted to be able to see the screen," his mother, Maureen Lynch, said. So they compromised, putting the machine in the hallway outside his room. From this roost, he chats online, looks at sports Web sites and plays an array of video games. Most of them, he said, are "pretty gory." ("Family Guidance Can Blunt the Effect of Video Violence," *New York Times*, September 25, 2000).

What's the issue here? Why is Will's mother concerned? What might Will be up to on the Web? Or worse, what might some not-so-nice people be up to out there in cyberspace, setting traps for Will and his brothers, sisters, and neighborhood pals? (And the neighborhood, by the way, thanks to the new technology, is now not just around the corner but around the world.)

Why are parents worried not only about the Internet, but about video games, tapes, films, and all sorts of things that are finding their way into the minds of the wide-eyed young through the ubiquitous screens, monitors, and cell phones that attract young eyes much in the way that moths are drawn to flame? Talk about not talking to strangers! Parents now have worldwide worries in this new dot-com day that dawned not all that long ago.

Parents will always have the problem of figuring out where trust ends and neglect begins in the matter of supervising their youngsters. Curious, isn't it? That the computer screen unit is called a monitor and the issue bothering Will Lapedes's mother in the news story just cited deals with monitoring what Will is doing in front of a monitor! The compromise solution is a transparency or sunshine solution so often applied to business, political, and professional ethics questions: Keep it out in the open, in the hallway where all can see what's on the screen.

The millstone awaits those out there in cyberspace and those in the studios and in the marketing and management divisions of the entertainment media who are literally scandalizing—causing to sin—the "little ones" of the world. Not just children, but the weak, the confused and curious, the less-than-mature believers who are being trapped, pulled down, and yanked away from God. Putting an obstacle between a little one and his or her God is another way of saying scandal, a modern example of activity that merits the millstone.

But it is not up to us to chop off hands, or cut off feet, or pull out others' eyes, not even metaphorically. It is not our job to tie the millstone around the offender's neck. It is not really our job to censor (although parents should indeed monitor, be on the alert, and attend to their supervisory responsibilities). Our job as a band of believers in a larger society, my friends, is to do all we can to confront what concerns us in this area, namely sex and violence, with workable entertainment alternatives. Just think of this for a moment: What if love and courage were to displace sex and violence in the entertainment media? I'm not suggesting that the undesirable stuff can be eliminated altogether (as worthy a goal as that surely is); we know it isn't going to happen. But what if we substitute creativity for censorship and what if we take whatever steps we can to stimulate the production of stories, films, plays, games, and entertaining images that portray genuine courage (not mindless violence) and genuine love (not exploitative, sensationalized sex)?

USA Today reported (September 28, 2000) that "Hollywood executives, under tense questioning from a Senate committee, said publicly for the first time that they targeted R-rated movie marketing to children. But while appearing to varying degrees contrite, some of the eight studio executives flatly refused to stop certain practices denounced in a Federal Trade Commission report [that prompted the hearing]."

Good for the Senate! Good for the Federal Trade Commission! Let's hope that they stimulate a keener sense of social responsibility in the executive ranks. When the Federal Trade Commission was set up in 1914, then-President Woodrow Wilson said that its preferred strategy in the face of objectionable business practice would be to "punish with pitiless publicity." Let's hope the FTC will keep the searchlight on the problem. But what might the rest of us do when the publicity comes to our attention? You'll have to answer that in specific terms for yourselves. I simply want to suggest that all of us have to become more interested in creativity—the creative arts, creative writing, creative advertising and marketing, and indeed creative thinking about the integration of both love and courage into our entertainment media.

Why can't love and courage displace sex and violence in the creative imaginations of those who produce the fare that feeds the minds of moviegoers and Internet surfers? Money is a very large part of the answer to that question, and so is human curiosity.

Follow the trail of dollars to pick up a few more clues. Dollars paid for products of the imagination are, for the most part, traceable to bookstore, magazine, box-office, and online sales, and to advertising revenue derived from anticipated sales to consumers. Giving people what they want at retail generates the dollars that deliver products designed to give them what they want in entertainment.

Many clearly want sex and violence; most do not. And those who don't cannot be dismissed as repressed, rigid, or religious zealots. More often than not, they are balanced human beings who, as children, heard and read good stories, learned to love good literature in their formal education, and maintained a reading habit for the rest of their lives.

If most Americans don't want sex and violence in entertainment for themselves and their children, why are sex and violence burying love and courage in popular entertainment? There is a national referendum on that question every day. Ballots are cast at newsstands, bookstores, box offices, as well as in clicks to cable channels, and hits in cyberspace.

Raunchy and gory images will not prevail over good taste in entertainment unless good people simply refuse to vote with their dollars in this culture contest. As happens in the political process, low voter participation permits relatively few citizens to control the outcome. In the entertainment market, a spending minority can define the culture downward. Curiosity drives a lot of this minority balloting, but I would argue that creativity could attract and hold the wandering eye now drawn to material that most of us find offensive.

Creativity can, I believe, draw entertainment expenditures out of the pockets of the now-passive majority, if worthy products are made available. But good entertainment products will not emerge unless creativity is appreciated. Moreover, worthy products will not emerge unless creativity is cultivated now at home and in the schools.

Censorship is not the answer. Attractive, creative programming is. Denunciation of inferior fare will never be an effective substitute for positive steps taken to encourage and reward creativity. Talk to yourself and among yourselves about what those positive steps might be. The poets, writers, and artists among you will surely have some ideas. The editors, producers, managers, and grant makers can certainly help. Legislators and regulators can encourage the process. Investment bankers and other investors can make a difference. All of us can pray.

And pray we must so that the millstone remedy will remain on the shelf as the objectionable material sinks of its own dead weight—an outcome, as one of civilization's most creative pens put it centuries ago, an outcome or "a consummation devoutly to be wished."

60

Twenty-Seventh Sunday of the Year

Genesis 2:18–24; Psalm 128; Hebrews 2:9–11; Mark 10:2–16

DIVORCE AND ANNULMENTS

"The Pharisees approached Jesus and asked, 'Is it lawful for a husband to divorce his wife?' They were testing him."

This Gospel passage is testing all of us, my friends. It challenges us to consider today, in the light of our Catholic faith, the troubling, painful question of divorce. We are also challenged in these modern times, to try to understand the relatively new phenomenon of annulments in the Catholic Church. I approach these questions cautiously, with no pleasure, and with no small degree of trepidation. I raise these questions only because this Gospel story demands serious reflection on the part of all of us who take the Gospel seriously.

Moses permitted divorce, the Pharisees reminded Jesus, but Jesus responded to them by saying: What Moses permitted for them and their forbearers to do in this regard was permitted only because of their hardness of heart. Then Jesus went on to say that God's intent, from the beginning of creation, was this: "What God had joined together [in marriage], no human being must separate." And we are left to puzzle over the questions of annulment and divorce in our day, and indeed, for some of us, in our own families and our own lives. These are difficult questions because they are so personal, and so often painful. But consider them we must.

The *New York Times Book Review* had a headline on October 1, 2000, (10) that read: "The Price of Divorce" and under it this sentence: "It's still the children who pay, and a new study says they go on paying well into adulthood." The book under review, *The Unexpected Legacy of Divorce* (New York: Hyperion) reports on the research of Judith

Wallerstein who, according to the reviewer, "more than anyone else has made us face the truth that a divorce can free one or both parents to start a new and more hopeful life and still hurt their children." That, of course, is one reason why this issue is so painful to discuss—the impact on children. It was made all the more painful for me recently when I heard an observer remark that so many college students today are "walking over the broken glass of their parents' marriages."

There are serious scholarly arguments pro and con on this point—the impact of divorce on the children. We know that, and we remain uneasy in the face of mounting divorce rates and annulment applications.

Even if there were no deleterious effect on the children, there is still emotional trauma in any divorce. And that is compounded for us Catholics by the Church's ban on remarriage for a divorced Catholic once validly married, whose former spouse still lives. This Gospel story offers little comfort to those thus situated, and the opening words from today's first reading from the Book of Genesis might well be heard as a taunt rather than a reassuring message by those for whom divorce was the best solution to a failed marriage: "The Lord God said: 'It is not good for the man to be alone. I will make a suitable partner for him.'" That partner, you should note, would come not from Adam's foot or head (where domination might be inferred), but from his rib, the region of the heart. That partner would be, by God's plan, the solution to the aching pain of loneliness. Hence the tragedy of the situation where the freedom granted by a divorce decree becomes, in fact, a sentence to the need for companionship, not a sentence to solitude, which is a chosen form of isolation, but to loneliness and the unsatisfied need for companionship.

Let me turn your attention then to the question of annulments. They are so easily misunderstood. "The most common misperception that exists [in this regard] is that a declaration of nullity denies that something existed. . . . [W]hen a marriage is declared null, the Church does not say that nothing existed. It says that what did exist was not what the Church means by marriage." There was a legal relationship, to be sure. There was a shared life, shared participation in good times and bad. More often than not, children were born of this union. But "what

222

existed did not fulfill the Church's requirements for marriage.... Something was missing from the very beginning that prevented this particular relationship from being what the Church calls 'marriage'" ("Splitsville: An Expert on Annulment Describes the Spiritual Consequence of Love among the Ruins," by Rev. Patrick R. Lagges, *Loyola— Alumni Magazine of Loyola University of Chicago* [Summer, 1998], 34).

What *is* required, what must be there right from the beginning for the Church to recognize the relationship as a marriage? There must be freedom on the part of bride and groom to enter into the contract; if there is coercion, there is no marriage contract. There must be no fraud; neither party can be bound by a previous marriage. There must be the physical capacity to consummate the marriage. There must be a commitment on the part of both bride and groom to the permanence of this marriage and to fidelity within the marriage. There must be openness to procreation, or, to put it another way, there must not be an intention to exclude altogether the possibility of having children. And just as the absence of physical capacity would mean no marriage, so the absence, at the outset, of the psychological capacity to assess with an appropriate degree of maturity what the marriage project requires of a person (and indeed marriage is a lifelong project!) would be grounds for declaring a marriage null. No psychological capacity— no maturity to appreciate reasonably and adequately at the outset what the demands will be—then, the Church will say, there was no marriage.

The annulment process looks back to the beginning of the marriage, to the presence or absence of these essential elements that had to be there if the reality that surely existed was, in fact, recognizable by the Church as a marriage. The retrospective examination in the annulment process of the failed relationship, going back to the beginning, is a review of the quality of the promise on which the marriage was built— "I promise to be good to you in good times and in bad, in sickness and in health, in riches and in poverty, until death." I'll return to that promise in a moment. But first, what about the children when the issue of annulment arises?

A question frequently asked by parents considering an annulment is: If the marriage was not really a marriage, are the children not really our children? Here is how a canon lawyer, who is experienced in marriage tribunal work, answers that question: "Church law specifically states that if the parents seemed to be in a valid marriage, then the children born of that marriage are considered legitimate. In Church law, legitimacy is something that you can acquire, but can never lose. Once you are considered legitimate, you are always considered legitimate, [e]ven if later on the marriage is declared null" (Lagges, 35).

But what about the psychological impact of a nullity declaration on the children of that marriage, once thought to be valid and now no longer recognized as such? Older children will want to know why the annulment is being sought. Adolescent and younger children will see this as a form of abandonment, a parent's choice to distance him- or herself from the child. The petitioning parent—that is, the one seeking the annulment—bears a special responsibility to provide a loving, unbiased, honest explanation. This responsibility can be made all the more manageable to the extent that the parent understands and is able to communicate what I'm attempting to explain here—the meaning of an annulment.

It is also helpful, even if it hurts, to recall the sacramental nature of what the Church calls marriage. Sacraments effect what they signify. The sacrament of marriage signifies God's faithful, fruitful, and abiding love for the Christian community. If there was inadequate intent, right from the beginning, with respect to fidelity, fruitfulness, and permanence; if there was insufficient freedom; if there was inadequate maturity—insufficient psychological capacity to undertake this awesome and holy responsibility—then there was an inadequate pledge on the part of two people, who may well have been in love, to commit their lives together as a sacramental sign of God's faithful, fruitful, and abiding presence in our world.

Let me come at this question one last time, and now from a completely secular source: the middle of the second act of Thornton Wilder's play, *The Skin of Our Teeth*. I find this helpful in focusing on the importance of the promise upon which a solid marriage rests.

Her husband has just told Mrs. Antrobus that he is leaving and will marry another woman. The stage directions have her recite the following speech "calmly, almost dreamily" as she says: "I didn't marry you because you were perfect, George. I didn't even marry you because I loved you. I married you because you gave me a promise. That promise made up for all your faults. And the promise I gave you made up for mine. Two imperfect people got married and it was the promise that made the marriage."

Well, dear friends, no one is perfect. It is always a pair of imperfect people who are there at the beginning and all the way through every marriage. The Church does its best to help them prepare to make the promise and keep it. The sacraments are sources of strength in keeping that promise. And the Church tries as best it can, in the midst of the difficult realities we've been reflecting on this morning, to be understanding and supportive of those who are struggling with the promise.

Renew that promise today, those of you who are married. Pray for the strength and clarity of purpose to make that promise one day, those of you who are looking forward to marriage. If you are a widow or widower, thank God for the years of marriage your promise made possible. And those of you who are separated or divorced, entrust yourselves now to God who cannot be anything but faithful to you, and whose grace will heal you in your hurts and broken places, as his love leads you along the path of peace.

61

Twenty-Eighth Sunday of the Year

Wisdom 7:7–11; Psalm 90; Hebrews 4:12–13; Mark 10:17–30

THROUGH THE EYE OF THE NEEDLE

Do you worry from time to time about how or whether you are going to make it "through the eye of the needle?" You heard Jesus say in today's Gospel reading that "it is easier for a camel to pass through the eye of a needle than for one who is rich to enter the kingdom of God." Upon hearing those words, most of us feel grateful that we are neither rich nor a member of the camel community. But those words should, nonetheless, give us pause.

True, Jesus is using a bit of hyperbole here; he is exaggerating—to make an important point—the difficulty of making it home to heaven if you are the prisoner of your possessions. If there is anything in your life that you refuse to surrender to the Lord, you do not possess it; it possesses you. And if that is the case with your material possessions, then today's Gospel invites you to examine your situation carefully.

Today's Gospel also makes another important point about following Christ, about discipleship, about vocation. The man who ran up to Jesus and asked what he must do in order to "inherit eternal life," was told about the essentials—the commandments. When he modestly asserted that "all of these [commandments] I have observed from my youth," Jesus looked at him with love and said, "You are lacking in one thing. Go sell what you have, and give to the poor and you will have treasure in heaven; then come, follow me."

Let me try today, dear friends, to weave these two points together— (1) making it through the eye of the needle and (2) responding to Christ's words, "follow me"—to join these two points in the context of a primitive Church document. This document dates back to the year

150. It describes what the early Christian community, gathered then as you are gathered now, did on Sunday. The author is a man known as Justin Martyr, an early saint who, as a member of a worshipping community in the earliest days of the Church, kept a journal and recorded for posterity what that community did on "the day that is named after the sun." I shall read a few paragraphs from that journal now, but let me say first that surely some in that early assembly, like some of you, were worried about making it "through the eye of the needle." And at least one in the community you will meet in just a moment, answered the "follow me" call by seeking ordained ministry for service as a priest to a faith community.

A Christian vocation is part of the life of every Christian—male and female, rich and poor, educated or not. You are, each one of you, a vocation. God has called you from the moment of your conception to be and to do, for his honor and glory, in the ordinary circumstances of your working life. Your answer to the "follow me" invitation may, in God's good providence for you, be firm and irrevocable; it has put you where you are in life. Or, that decision may not yet have been made firmly; your options may still be open. And although, as I hope you clearly understand, I do not narrow the meaning of the word "vocation" to mean only a vocation to the priesthood, I do today want to ask those young men whose options are still open, to consider a vocation to priesthood as you listen to this account, written in the year 150, from the pen of Justin Martyr:

On the day that is named after the sun, all who dwell in the towns and surrounding countryside gather together for a communal celebration. And then the memoirs of the Apostles or the writings of the Prophets are read, as long as time permits. After the reader has finished, the one presiding gives an address, urgently admonishing all to practice these beautiful teachings in their lives. Then all stand up and pray together. And at the end of the prayers… the bread and wine mixed with water are brought forward, and the president offers up prayers and thanksgivings, to the best of his ability. And the people express their approval by saying Amen. Then takes place the distribution, to all present, of the things over which the thanksgiving had been spoken, and the deacons take a portion to the absent. Moreover, those who are well-to-do contribute whatever they wish. The collection is deposited with the president of the assembly who uses it to help widows and orphans, and those who, through sickness or any other cause, are in want, and those who are in bonds, and the strangers sojourning among us, and in a word takes care of all who are in need. But Sunday is the day on which we all hold our common assembly, because it is the first day on which God made the world; and Jesus Christ our Savior on the same day rose from the dead.

Sound familiar? The readings from Scripture, the homily, offering of the gifts, the eucharistic prayer and the great Amen, communion for all present, the never-to-be-omitted collection (!), communion to the sick and homebound, and the use of financial resources for social ministry and works of mercy.

Where are those people now, the gathered assembly of believers that Justin described, where are they now? With the Lord, of course. How can we be so sure of that? Because they were there, Sunday after Sunday, in the channel that leads to salvation; the same channel where you are today.

So, are you worried about making it through the eye of the needle? Have faith. If in a couple of hundred years from now, someone were to find a description of what this gathered community did on this Sunday in this place and asked that same question—Where are they now?—they would surely answer, "with the Lord," because "they" (in this case you) were in their own time on earth in that same channel of grace that leads to eternal life. You were giving praise and thanks on Sunday and remembering the Lord in the breaking of the bread, just as the people Justin described were doing centuries ago.

You are linked with them in the history of salvation, that link will hold for life everlasting if—and there is, of course an important if—you don't get weighed down by wealth to the point of breaking away from the loving God who wills salvation for you, who died that you might live, and, and this is the second if, if members of the faith community continue to present themselves for ordained ministry in response to the call, "Follow me." Note that when the young man in today's Gospel story heard Jesus narrate the conditions of discipleship, "his face fell, and he went away sad, for he had many possessions." He walked away, took a hike, left it to others to answer the call for ministerial service to the community.

Mysteriously, our God is a God in need of help. He needs all of us to minister to one another in some fashion, he needs relatively few of us to preside at the assembly, to be priests in service to the faith community and the world beyond.

Notice that the fellow who failed to exercise this option, "went away sad." Would he have been happier had he responded affirmatively to the invitation? Quite probably. Would he have been "worthy" of the call? Certainly not. Would he have fit the following reflection of Karl Rahner on the priesthood? (I'll read it in a moment.) I suspect he would and I hope those in whose hearts these words rings a bell will talk to one of us priests about priesthood. We would be privileged to try to help you discern God's will for you, your vocation according to God's plan. In any case, listen for a moment to these words of Karl Rahner, the late great German Jesuit theologian:

The priest is not an angel sent from heaven.
He is a man, a member of the Church, a Christian.
Remaining man and Christian, he begins to speak to you the word of God.
This word is not his own. No, he comes to you because God has told him to proclaim God's word.
Perhaps he has not entirely understood it himself. Perhaps he adulterates it. Perhaps he falters and stammers. How else could he speak God's word, ordinary man that he is?
But must not some one of us say something about God, about eternal life, about the majesty of grace in our sanctified being; must not some one of us speak of sin, the judgment and mercy of God?

You young men who still have your options open, give those words some prayerful thought.

May all of us, as a parish community, help each other engage in any weight-reduction programs that might be necessary if we are to make it through the eye of the needle. Let us also pray with thanks for those ordained ministers who surrendered a measure of their personal freedom in order to serve, to keep open for us access to the channel of salvation, the Eucharist. And let us earnestly pray for those young men in our midst who may be considering the call to ordained ministry as their best personal response to the "Follow me" invitation.

Let me close with a few wise words from the late Fr. Eugene Walsh, a great Sulpician priest, who was fond of saying to people of all ages and states in life the following words that would have been applicable in Justin's time and are certainly applicable to you today, "Christ promises you two important things: your life can have real meaning and you are going to live with him forever. If you can get a better offer, take it."

62

Twenty-Ninth Sunday of the Year

Isaiah 53:10–11; Psalm 33; Hebrews 4:14–16; Mark 10:35–45

NOT TO BE SERVED, BUT TO SERVE

Dear friends, you just heard a one-sentence summary of the mission of Jesus Christ. You heard him say to the Twelve: "For the Son of Man did not come to be served but to serve, and to give his life as a ransom for many." "Many" means "all," the entire human race; the "Son of Man" is a messianic title, an expression that occurs seventy times in the Synoptic Gospels; in every case, Jesus applies the title to himself. It is precisely as Son of Man, a title that emphasizes his humanity, that Jesus suffers and dies. That title puts him close to you. The second person of the Holy Trinity, he who had nothing whereby he could die, took upon himself a human nature in order to suffer and die for us, because we, in our sinful humanity, had nothing whereby we could live. He had to become Son of Man if we were to be saved.

"The Son of Man did not come to be served but to serve, and to give his life as a ransom for many." If you want to understand Christ, you have to understand service. If you are interested in salvation, you have to be interested in service. If you want to be like Christ, you have to be concerned about serving, not being served.

Let's talk about service today. I invite you to think about service. I urge you today to pray about service. If you want to find a key to happiness, take a look at service. If you become more concerned about meeting the needs of others than in having your own needs met, you will have off-loaded the burden of selfishness and taken a sure step in the lighter, brighter direction of service. Service is turning your talents inside out—putting your gifts at the disposal of others. Service is sacrifice—extending yourself, stretching out a helping hand toward others in need, translating love from easy and possibly empty words into meaningful deeds.

Consider your past education, training, and experience as a "seasoning" for service, a credentialing for service, a conditioning and formal positioning of yourself to be of service to others in the human community. Service with a smile? Why not? Military service? Maybe. Secret Service? Perhaps. Social Service? That's a possibility. Customer service? Again, an occupational possibility. Legal services, medical services, an Internet Service Provider, government service, business services, or simply service through business—wherever you happen to be in the world of work, for-profit or not-for-profit activity, community service, volunteer service; wherever you sit or stand in the organizational hierarchy—at the top, or at the bottom, or anywhere in between—you can serve. You can break out of your self-centeredness, you can overcome your isolation and loneliness, you can make a difference in the life of others and in your own life through service.

About twenty years ago, I received a phone call from a senior in one of the nation's premier universities. She is the daughter of close friends of mine. She considers me as a quasi-uncle. She called for help. She opened the phone conversation by saying, "Everyone here is rich and unhappy. Can you help me find an overseas service opportunity that will help me cut through all this after I graduate?" She was onto something. I helped. She volunteered, did some good, returned home to career, marriage, and family. She found happiness through service.

On October 19, 2000, the *New York Times* ran an interesting story under this headline, "Geeks, Proud of the Name, Start a Volunteer Corps." Listen to a few lines from this story:

> Sara Wustner, a Seattle software engineer, thought about joining the Peace Corps when she graduated from the University of California at San Diego in 1998. But, she said, "they didn't have anything that really fit my skills."
>
> Now, with a stint at Microsoft on her resume, she has taken a leave of absence from her job at Oxygen Media to live in Ghana for three months. Ms. Wustner is part of the pilot team of six volunteers for Geekcorps, a high tech version of the Peace Corps.

Instead of teaching math, as technologically adept Peace Corps workers often do, Ms. Wustner, 24, will help a Ghanaian software company teach its workers the Java and Unix programming languages.

"I want the satisfaction of feeling that all of the expensive education that I got helped someone in a really real way," she said.

This new form of venture philanthropy, my friends, is just another example of the oldest, so-often-tried, and unfailingly true remedy for drift and purposelessness, and that remedy is, of course, service.

Looking for purpose in your life? (That's just another way of asking if you are searching for meaning in your life.) If you are looking for purpose, try service. This is not to say that you have to go to Ghana to find it. Look around right where you are—in the setting and circumstances where the call of Christ may well have placed you—right there where you are now, look for opportunities to serve. Whether you serve supper or serve a subpoena, whether it's a form of customer services or financial services, your service can be a reincarnation in your own space and time of him who came "not to be served but to serve and to give [his] life as a ransom for many."

Are you interested in being or becoming a leader? Then begin right now to write your autobiography in lines of service to those you want to lead. Are you asking yourself whether or not you have the potential to lead? You can start answering that question by presenting any evidence you can find of significant service in your life up till now. And you will find, by the way, in your own life and the lives of truly great leaders, that the more significant the service, the more likely that the source of that service will be rooted in simplicity. The simpler the source, the greater the leadership. Isn't that certainly the case with Christ, "meek and humble of heart," who is arguably the greatest leader who ever lived?

If you want to lead, show your willingness to be available, accountable, and vulnerable; this triad—availability, accountability, and vulnerability—qualify you for what Robert Greenleaf has called *Servant Leadership*. Take a look at his book by that title (from Paulist Press) and you'll find a gold mine of useful information not typically found in the MBA curriculum, but indispensable for both success and faithful discipleship on the part of the Christian manager/leader in the modern corporation or organization.

Jesus Christ, MBA? Jesus Christ, CEO? I know books and articles have been written under those titles, but I'm not talking about that. I'm talking about you the Christian and Christ your model. You heard the prophet Isaiah's words in the first reading today, words applied by the Church to Jesus: "The Lord was pleased to crush him in infirmity. If he gives his life as an offering for sin, he shall see his descendants in a long life, and the will of the Lord shall be accomplished through him." You are among those descendants. Your service is part of his accomplishment.

"Brothers and sisters," today's reading from the Letter to the Hebrew's said, "Since we have a great high priest who has passed through the heavens, Jesus, the Son of God, let us hold fast to our confession. For we do not have a high priest who is unable to sympathize with our weaknesses, but one who has similarly been tested in every way, yet without sin. So let us confidently approach the throne of grace to receive mercy and to find grace for timely help."

Mercy indeed; timely help you can count on. You can count on all the help you will need so that you, like him, can go forth from this place to serve, and not to be served, and to give your life in the way he would have you give it—in partnership with him for the ransom of many, for the salvation of the world.

63

Thirtieth Sunday of the Year

Jeremiah 31:7–9; Psalm 126; Hebrews 5:1–6; Mark 10:46–52

PITY, COURAGE, FAITH

The Church invites you to give some thought today to the gift of faith—to the reality of faith in your life. The Gospel reading from Mark puts a nice incentive in front of you; toward the end of today's reading you heard Jesus say, "[Y]our faith has saved you." You know you can't be saved by faith alone, but you also know that works alone won't do it either and that without faith you cannot reap the fruits of the redemption won for you by Christ. So hear him say again to you today, "Your faith has saved you," and give thanks for the great gift of faith.

What is faith? Don't think of faith as a recitation of propositions about God. Think of faith as the act and attitude by which you entrust yourself to God. There is content to it, of course, but there is a disposition too.

If an image might be helpful, go back for a moment to your childhood memory of "the greatest show on earth," the circus, and recall your mounting excitement as you watched a performer swing on one trapeze in rhythm with an empty trapeze swinging toward and away from the artist as both swung high above a net. Drums rolled. Anticipation heightened. The performer eventually let go of the trapeze bar on which he or she had been swinging and, after a midair moment of no support at all, caught onto the empty trapeze that carried him or her up to a secure ledge from which the artist took a bow and received your applause. Faith is like that moment of letting go and catching on. You are sure—by faith—that God will catch you; you "let go"—in an act of faith—relying, not on a safety net below, but on a faithful, loving God above.

Play the role of Bartimaeus, the blind man, today. He is the blind beggar in this Gospel story who heard that Jesus of Nazareth was coming down the road toward him and he shouted out, "Jesus, son of David, have pity on me."

Who among us has no need of the divine pity? Who among us is without blind spots? Who among us would not want to say, "Jesus, son of David, have pity on me?" Say it silently in prayer today; try saying it in your colloquy with Jesus at communion time. Your sophistication may, like the advance men and traffic handlers depicted in this Gospel story, "rebuke" you and tell you "to be silent," but take a page from the Bartimaeus book and keep "calling out all the more," "Son of David, have pity on me."

What did Jesus do? He told the leaders of the gathered crowd to call the blind man over for a face-to-face encounter. And as they called Bartimaeus to come to Jesus, these bystanders offered very sound advice: "Take courage; get up, Jesus is calling you." Take courage he did, as you should do, and he "sprang up," as you, propelled by faith should also do, and you will hear Jesus say to you, as he said to Bartimaeus, "What do you want me to do for you?"

"What do you want me to do for you?" Don't take that question lightly; don't let it slip from your consciousness. Don't for a moment think that Jesus is not serious when he asks, "What do you want me to do for you?" Yes, you, good old you, little old you, bad old you—however worthy or unworthy you consider yourself to be—he is asking you, "What do you want me to do for you?"

Your response must in some way or other echo the response of Bartimaeus, "Master, that I may see." Sure, you should specify, you should particularize your response, your request. Ask for anything you want, but focus on a genuine need and when you mention it to the Lord, ask first for a cure of any blind spots that might be troubling you, that might be making it difficult for you "to see" God's will. "Master, that I may see" is a petition all of us should be making. With clearer spiritual vision, we will come to see our true needs. We will more readily accept whatever it is that God positively wills for us or simply permits to come our way because of God's refusal to override our freedom when we use that freedom unwisely. Similarly, God will not ordinarily interfere with the freedom of others who may use their freedom badly to harm us. We can and should, of course, pray for protection from all harm, and for vision sufficiently clear to see harm when it is headed our way. We should pray to be kept, by circumstance and choice, out of harm's way, so far as that is possible.

The important thing is a cure for our blind spots. Pray for that as you say, with Bartimaeus, "Master, that I may see." And you can count on hearing Jesus say to you, "Go your way; your faith has saved you." What a gift!

It is all there for you in this beautiful Gospel story—pity, courage, faith. The divine pity is yours; you can count on it. The grace of courage is yours; you can act on it. And the gift of faith is yours, for which you can be nothing but grateful as you "go your way," keeping your eye of faith fixed on the will of God.

64

Thirty-First Sunday of the Year

Deuteronomy 6:2–6; Psalm 18; Hebrews 7:23–28; Mark 12:28–34

THE GREATEST COMMANDMENT

The question has been around for a long, long time; here it is again in today's Gospel selection: "Which is the first of all the commandments?" One of the scribes asked the question; it was directed, of course, to Jesus.

Now there were a lot of commandments around in those days. You get a hint of that from today's first reading, the selection you heard from the Book of Deuteronomy, where Moses told the people to fear the Lord and keep "all his statutes and commandments…and thus have long life." Moses didn't give a precise number of exactly how many "statutes and commandments" there were, but if you take a look at the Book of Deuteronomy (that word, by the way, means "Second Law"), you'll be impressed. And it is to the Book of Deuteronomy that Jesus turns by way of reply to the question presented to him by the unnamed scribe in today's Gospel. Jesus says: "This is the first [commandment]: 'Hear, O Israel! The Lord our God is Lord alone! Therefore, you shall love the Lord your God with all your heart, with all your soul, with all your mind, and with all your strength.'" [That's Deuteronomy 6:4–5.] And Jesus goes on to say, "And this is the second, 'You shall love your neighbor as yourself.' There is no other commandment greater than these."

Love—love of God and love of neighbor—love is at the pinnacle and at the core of all our obligations. Love is what we are commanded to do. Love should be our defining characteristic.

Now notice that today's Gospel reaches back into what we call the Old Testament, the old Law, the Torah. What Jesus specifies here as the "greatest" of all the commandments puts us on common ground with our Jewish brothers and sisters, with those who live by the Old Testament. This law of love applies to them as well as to those who follow Christ.

So let me speak of love today and let me suggest, as we begin this reflection, that it might be appropriate for us to examine the extent to which we love our Jewish brothers and sisters, as well as taking a moment to measure the extent of our love for those who follow the tenets of the third Abrahamic religion, Islam. All three of these religions preach love. The world would be a far better place if followers of the three monotheistic Abrahamic religions—Judaism, Christianity, and Islam—really loved one another, as indeed they are all commanded to do. But back to the notion of love.

What is love?

The word means many things to many people. Popular culture debases it in song and story; great literature and great lives display its profound beauty. At bottom, love is sacrifice. It is the willingness to lay down one's life for another.

What you heard a moment ago when Jesus said that the second great commandment is to love your neighbor as you love yourself, that too comes from the old Law, the Old Testament. Keeping in mind that love is sacrifice, that love is the willingness to lay down your life for another, and recalling that Jesus laid down his life for you, you have a delicate and careful step to take to prevent yourself from becoming an Old Testament Christian, which, of course, would be something of a contradiction in terms.

You will recall that, in his farewell discourse, communicated to us in the Gospel of John (13:34), Jesus said: "I give you a new commandment; love one another as I have loved you." "Love one another, as I have loved you." There is something new here.

This is a new commandment. The old commandment, the old Law was, "Love your neighbor as you love yourself." Jesus the rabbi, the teacher, early in his public life as we encounter him here in today's Gospel story, quoted that old Law, that old commandment, when he was asked about the requirements of the Law. When the question was asked, there was only the one Law, what we now call the old Law.

But at the Last Supper, you have Jesus the priest on the night he instituted both the Eucharist and the priesthood—Jesus the priest at the first Mass, begun in the upper room and completed on the cross—there at the Last Supper Jesus gave his followers a new law, a new commandment. They can no longer be content to love their neighbors as they love themselves (the old Law). It is no longer sufficient to "do unto others, as you would have them do unto you." No, the new commandment requires you to love one another—in his words— "as I have loved you."

"As I have done for you, you should also do" (John 13:15).

Love is shown in deeds, not words, deeds like washing the feet of the apostles as Jesus did at the Last Supper. And on the next day, there would be another deed, he would lay down his life for all of humanity.

"Love one another, as I have loved you," said Jesus. For us, that means love one another as Christ loved you—to the point of laying down your life for one another. "By this will all men and women know that you are my disciples, that you love one another," says Jesus just a little later in his farewell discourse (John 13:35). There is no greater love that anyone can have than to lay down your life for another, Jesus said. He intended this to be a revolutionary doctrine. He hoped by word and example to bring about a change of heart, an attitudinal turnaround in his followers. He is talking here about love.

Jesus taught by word and example a strategy for a revolution that is, for all practical purposes, yet to begin. Take a look around you and what do you see in your immediate surroundings, in this city, in the United States of America, in the world? Do you see love, or hate, or just indifference? Do you see people tripping over one another to be helpful, considerate, kind? Do you see foot-washers, sacrificers, and gracious givers? Or do you see people walking over one another in hard-hearted neglect—or worse?

The new commandment was intended to revolutionize human relations, quite literally to change the world. "Love one another, as I have loved you." "As I have done for you, you should also do." Be kind, be considerate, be Christian!

So when you think about the greatest commandment, think about love. And when you think about love, think about sacrifice. And when you think about sacrifice, remember that there is no greater love than to lay down your life for another. That's what Christ did for you. You can no longer be content to do unto others as they have done for you, or to love others as they love you. That's an ethic of reciprocity. You are called to an ethic of renunciation. That's what you are commanded to do—by virtue of the new commandment—you are called to lay down your lives for one another.

The world is waiting. Let the revolution begin!

65

Thirty-Second Sunday of the Year

1 Kings 17:10–16; Psalm 146; Hebrews 9:24–28; Mark 12:38–44

THE WIDOW'S MITE

Mahatma Ghandi once remarked, "There comes a time when an individual becomes irresistible and his action all-pervasive in its effect. This comes when he reduces himself to zero."

Today's Gospel story—the famous account of the widow's mite—deals with zero net worth. The story is known worldwide. Its lesson of freedom and generosity becomes, in many Christian hearts, "irresistible." Its salutary "effect" does indeed become "all-pervasive" in the lives of those who approach this story with deep Christian faith and draw from it inspiration to live simply and give generously.

Zero net worth. I talked not long ago with a former student, now a practicing accountant who does tax work. "I deal with high net worth individuals," he told me. No need for the widow in today's Gospel story to consult with him! But she may indeed have consulted with tradition, with her biblically based faith tradition. She may have known the story of another widow taken from the First Book of Kings, the story that was repeated for you to hear as the first reading in today's liturgy. The prophet Elijah, you will recall, came upon this woman as she was gathering sticks for a fire to cook a paltry meal. He called out to her, "Please bring me a small cupful of water to drink." And as she left to get it, he added, "Please bring along a bit of bread." She answered, "As the Lord, your God, lives, I have nothing baked; there is only a handful of flour in my jar and a little oil in my jug. Just now I was collecting a couple of sticks, to go in and prepare something for myself and my son; when we have eaten it, we shall die." This good woman is definitely not what anyone would call "a high net worth individual!"

But Elijah said to her: "Do not be afraid. Go and do as you propose. But first make me a little cake and bring it to me. Then you can prepare something for yourself and your son." Had he really heard her sad story? Was he listening? Is what we're seeing here a "let-me-eat-cake" salute to insensitivity? No, it was all part of God's plan. Elijah the prophet reminded her that "the Lord, the God of Israel says, 'The jar of flour shall not go empty, nor the jug of oil run dry, until the day when the Lord sends rain upon the earth.'"

So she left and dutifully did as Elijah had said. And the Scripture account proclaims: "She was able to eat for a year, and he and her son as well; the jar of flour did not go empty, nor the jug of oil run dry, as the Lord had foretold through Elijah."

It is just possible, is it not, that the poor widow of today's Gospel story was familiar with this story. Through this story, she may well have been introduced to the curious celestial arithmetic that we see to be at work in the mind of Jesus as he sat there "opposite the [temple] treasury and observed how the crowd put money into the treasury." Listen again to Mark's account: "Many rich people put in large sums. A poor widow also came and put in two small coins worth a few cents. Calling his disciples to himself, he said to them, 'Amen, I say to you, this poor widow put in more than all the other contributors to the treasury.'" More? We've already been told that they—the rich—put in "large sums," but she put in a mite, a pittance, just two small coins. How can Jesus make the arithmetic work? How can he say that she put in "more than all the other contributors to the treasury?" Well, listen to his explanation: "For they have all contributed from their surplus wealth, but she, from her poverty, has contributed all she had, her whole livelihood."

In this case, less is more (and that is so often the case in those areas of life where matter and spirit meet, where faith and works converge, where you and your Creator God meet as question and answer in your search for a solution to the riddle of life). In this inspired puzzle, Mark lays out for you a lesson that says your generosity is measured against your capacity. If your net worth is zero and you still give, a wonderful multiplication takes place. The arithmetic is on your side. Your less is a whole lot more. Why? Because God is God and you simply cannot imagine the dimensions of God's loving and powerful providence. God will indeed provide!

Look at how the widow whom Elijah the prophet encountered fared. She gave away what little she had and, miraculously, she was able "to eat for a year, and her son as well." And this dear woman in today's Gospel story—unnamed but forever remembered—this dear widow gave her mite unhesitatingly, and with even less hesitation a loving God rewarded her in ways not recorded here. What we do know is that Jesus used her presence and her generosity to expose the hypocrisy of the scribes and the corruption of the institutional temple trappings that were stifling the spirit of true religion.

Jesus denounces the scribes in this Gospel story. They "devour the houses of widows," Jesus said, in order to maintain a corrupt temple system. Supporting the institution, supporting the system, keeps the widow poor! Jesus wanted to stand up for people, especially poor people, over and against the system. For the scribes, people were unimportant; it was the institutional religious system that really counted and the people could be exploited to keep the system going. Jesus denounced all that.

But we cannot afford to ignore the curious arithmetic—the way less can become more for those who believe in God. Those among us who are high net worth individuals should give all this some careful thought, as should those of any degree of positive net worth, high, middle or low.

Everyone should give according to his or her means. But there is a range, within one's means, that covers token gifts, stretch gifts, and sacrificial gifts. And the good example being offered in today's Gospel story suggests that token gifts just won't do. Stretch a bit. "Give till it hurts," as the saying goes. Don't be afraid to sacrifice.

Where or to whom should your stretch or sacrificial gifts be going? That's for you to decide. The Gospel guideline available for your consideration today would invite you to think before you give, think about the system your gift might be supporting.

Your parish has to take care to be worthy of your gifts. When you judge your parish not to be worthy of your stretch or sacrificial gift, don't just not give; tell your pastor where your parish is falling short.

Ten percent of what you give to this parish (Holy Trinity in Washington, DC) each week goes to worthy projects recommended by the parish's Social Justice Committee. The parish tithes to help the poor, to promote justice, and does so because faith requires it. It is not exactly the Robin Hood effect that is at work here because the parish doesn't steal from the rich to give to the poor. It is more like a conduit that receives from those who have in order to help those who have not. The parish can help those who exercise responsible stewardship. All of us are called to be faithful stewards.

The special needs we put before you from time to time will always be genuine needs. The causes we ask you to support—the second collections that come around each year for things like the Campaign for Human Development, Catholic Relief Services, Catholic Charities, and similar good causes—all give you an opportunity to stretch, if not to sacrifice. The zone between stretch and sacrifice is a matter of the heart—your heart and no one else's.

I was amused while in college to read Peter Finley Dunne's wry commentator, the Irish Mr. Dooley, observe that every time Andrew Carnegie made a philanthropic gesture it sounded like a waiter with a tray full of cocktail glasses falling down the stairs! Whether you stretch or sacrifice, be discreet and quiet about it. Be content not to have your left hand know what your right hand is doing. But, by all means, make sure that you are contributing something significant into this mix of celestial arithmetic that we've been considering today.

If you contribute nothing, the multiplication machine cannot get to work. If you contribute next to nothing, as did the widow in this Gospel story, your gift will multiply in direct proportion to the dent it places in your capacity to give. It will also, by God's good providence, keep you in oil and flour for the entire year! And if you contribute a lot, if you walk that extra mile, only you will know how good it feels to partner with God in the unfolding of the mysterious multiplication of the widow's mite.

66

Thirty-Third Sunday of the Year

Daniel 12:1–3; Psalm 16; Hebrews 10:11–14, 18; Mark 13:24–32

"LEARN A LESSON FROM THE FIG TREE"

The Church invites you to reflect today on the last things—on death, judgment, and life after death. You are invited to think, as Jesus invited his disciples in the Gospel reading to think, about the end time when "the sun will be darkened, and moon will not give its light, and the stars will be falling from the sky, and the powers in the heavens will be shaken." Scary thoughts.

But, at that very time, the end time, the Son of Man will come "in the clouds with great power and glory, and then he will send out the angels and gather his elect from the four winds"—from all points on the compass; in other words, he will gather his elect "from the end of the earth to the end of the sky." You are invited today to think big—really big; from the end of the earth to the end of the sky. What height! What breadth! What a stretch for your faith-based imagination.

This is indeed a very serious but not-so-scary thought, because it holds out to you the promise of salvation, of eternal security in the arms of God.

Jesus wants you to be ready. The Church each year at this time, the end of the liturgical year (the end of so-called "Ordinary Time") wants you to consider soberly and prayerfully the last things as they apply to you. So Jesus says to his disciples and the Church says to you: "Learn a lesson from the fig tree." Let's examine that lesson carefully.

The familiar growth pattern of a fig tree in spring and summer is presented here as a basis for comparison with the sequence of events leading up to the coming of the Son of Man. Notice that it is spring and summer—bright times, hopeful times—that are associated with

246

the natural growth process of the fig tree. Watch the greening, the springing forth, and you know that the fruit is on its way. Watch the darkening of sun and moon, see the stars falling, and you know that the Son of Man, Christ your Lord, is coming to take you to himself. Not so scary after all for those who are waiting, ready, and sufficiently perceptive to read the signs correctly.

It is understandable, of course, that the unknown raises fears in the human heart. It is not at all unusual to be frightened at the prospect of death. That is perfectly natural. It is also understandable that the prospect of the end of the world happening before one's eyes is enough to stir feelings of terror in a human heart. That is not the feeling Jesus wants you to experience now. Peace is his gift to you. Peace of heart in the midst of contingency and uncertainty is his gift to you, if you have faith enough to accept it.

Those who delight in superstition and who tend to be fundamentalists in matters religious, can frighten you with their predictions that the end is near. Those who like to think of themselves as blasé and sophisticated, and who might even identify themselves as not at all religious but quite this-worldly and secularized, can worry you if they seem to be completely oblivious to the lesson Jesus is trying to teach in today's Gospel. But most good people who are neither secularists nor fundamentalists, simply tend to brush these fearsome thoughts off with a nod to a very distant—billions of years from now distant—possibility that the world as we know it will all incinerate, disintegrate, or otherwise collapse, but that this will happen long after they are gone. Well, maybe.

But to where will they have gone? And when will they have experienced their personal end time, their unique disengagement, their separation from all that is familiar? When will they have met the final darkness and how, indeed, did they make their way through? In short, what happened when their number finally came up? We tend not to want to think about that.

Let me suggest to you today, dear friends, that you personalize all this, that you exercise your imagination to make yourself—your body, mind, and spirit—the center of your unique universe. If you are to learn the lesson of the fig tree, you are going to have to bring it much closer to home. Speaking of the fig tree, Jesus said, "When its branch becomes tender and sprouts leaves, you know that summer is near." That applied to you in infancy and the springtime of your life; just looking at yourself then (or others looking at you) it was obvious that summer was near.

Now, Jesus wants you to take an upside, bright side, brimming-with-hope perspective on your unique life experience when you see these other portents, when the sun and moon no longer give their light. Sure, you are virtually certain that these signs will not occur in your own time, but don't be so foolish as to ignore the signs that certainly do occur and are plainly visible in your mirror, in your energy level, your memory function, and which are unmistakably there when you advert for a moment to the date on your birth certificate. Read those signs of your times; face up to them. What are they saying to you?

They are saying that the coming of the Son of Man is closer for you now than ever before. For many of you, the signs of your times are saying that you are closer now to the end than to the beginning. How close? No one can say, but if the prospect of going home to a God who loves you has absolutely no appeal, you have to wonder about your belief in the fact that a heaven awaits you, that eternal union with God is yours for the taking. And you have to wonder about your gratitude to God who has done all this for you.

By connecting the sight of a growing, burgeoning, light-seeking fig tree to the dark signs of the end time, Jesus is telling you that your personal end time is a prelude to eternal happiness. Yet we are all so taken in by our secular culture's fascination, adulation, glamorization, even adoration of youth that we are embarrassed, ashamed, saddened by the signs of our own approaching end time. We foolishly consider aging, inevitable and unavoidable as it is, as some kind of failure. Granted, some of us did "let ourselves go," as the saying goes, and this is no compliment to our Creator. We can and should regret that. But all of us face limits. We diminish physically. We grow old. Nothing to be ashamed of. Nothing to try to deny. Regrettable somewhat, yes, but only because life is so good and our loves are so strong; we hate the thought of leaving this behind. Nonetheless, the end will inevitably come and the signs are not to be ignored.

That's the mood the Church encourages you to adopt today as Ordinary Time comes to an end. That's the perspective you should take as you prepare to experience the wonderful Advent expectancy again this year. That's the spiritual interpretation to put on the fallen leaves, the darker days, the autumn all around you, whether or not this calendar season coincides with the autumn or even winter of your own personal life.

I'm always amused and occasionally saddened when I meet someone recovering from surgery, or an accident, or serious illness and ask, "How are you doing?" only to hear them say, "Not bad, considering the alternative!" It causes me to wonder whether or not they have ever, in fact, considered the alternative. God has great things in store for you; read the signs of your own personal times as mileposts on a journey to eternal happiness that is coming closer every day. "But," as Jesus explained in today's Gospel, "of that day or hour no one knows, neither the angels in heaven, nor the Son, but only the Father."

So, dear friends, as the twenty-seventh Psalm puts it, "Wait for the Lord with courage; be stouthearted, and wait for the Lord." That's what it means to believe; that's what it means to be a Christian.

67

Thirty-Fourth or Last Sunday of the Year, Solemnity of Our Lord Jesus Christ, King of the Universe

Daniel 7:13–14; Psalm 93; Revelation 1:5–8; John 18:33–37

"MY KINGDOM DOES NOT BELONG TO THIS WORLD"

This is the Feast of Christ the King. It is the last Sunday of the liturgical year. We are approaching Advent—which is preparation time—but here we are at the end, on the last Sunday of the year, looking back, and listening to a very interesting exchange between Jesus and Pontius Pilate.

Listening in on this conversation between Jesus and Pilate will be instructive on the following three points: first, whether Jesus saw himself in any way as a king; second, what kind of a king he may have considered himself to be; and third, how we should view ourselves and conduct ourselves as followers of Christ the King.

The Gospels, as you know, were written long after Jesus had died. They are divinely inspired, we believe, but we also know they reflect the accumulated insights of early believers as they spoke to one another and handed down to their children and grandchildren stories about Jesus—what he did, what he said, how he conducted himself during his relatively short sojourn on earth. The written accounts came in the wake of what we call an oral tradition.

The four Gospels differ from one another in many particulars. Today's reading comes from the Fourth Gospel, the one attributed to John, and this Gospel is often referred to as more spiritual, more theological, than the others. Bear this in mind as you listen to the conversation between Jesus and Pilate, recalling as you listen, that words were put on the lips of Jesus by those who constructed the written accounts, which may not have been literally on his lips when he walked this earth. They are, nonetheless, inspired words. What you are listening in on here is what the Holy Spirit wants you to hear!

Point number one: Pilate opens the dialogue with a question: "Are you the King of the Jews?" What might Jesus have thought when he heard that word *king*? King Herod might have come to mind, but probably not; Jesus was not thinking in political or this-worldly terms. Surely, Jesus knew that he was not King Herod. He was, however, and knew that he was, a descendant of David who was a king. Might that have occurred to him as he entertained Pilate's question? There were lots of kings around in those days. It is unlikely that a carpenter from Nazareth had much interaction with kings so, I suspect, he would have thought of kingship in terms of leadership, not in terms of pomp and power. What might that term have meant to Jesus? We can assume that he took it to mean a leader, a person of strength and influence. And that's why, when he got around to answering the question, Jesus could say: "My kingdom does not belong to this world. If my kingdom did belong to this world, my attendants would be fighting to keep me from being handed over to the Jews. But as it is, my kingdom is not here." His leadership, his kingship, his strength was in an altogether different order from anything Pilate may have had in mind.

But Pilate continued to press the question: "So, then, you are a king?" And this sets Jesus up for a reply that leaves the kingship notion with Pilate while spelling out the style and dimensions of the leadership Jesus came to provide: "For this I was born and for this I came into the world, to testify to the truth. Everyone who belongs to the truth listens to my voice." And that puts Pilate pretty much out of the conversation. Why? Because Pilate was not committed to the truth. Jesus was. And so must those be who would follow Jesus, who might look upon him as a king.

Moving on now to our second point, we can examine more closely the question of what kind of a king Jesus might have considered himself to be. For some help on this, I am going to take you to the book of the *Spiritual Exercises* of St. Ignatius Loyola, a handbook outline of mediations and contemplations designed to help a person at prayer come to a better understanding of God's will for him or her. Ignatius has a famous meditation on the "Call of Christ the King." And he begins his portrayal of Christ by first presenting a description of an ideal earthly king—a leader everyone respects and admires. This human king, as Ignatius portrays him, is chosen by God and because he is called by God, "all Christian princes and people pay [him] homage and obedience."

He has a mission and he explains it to his people in terms that will certainly sound strange to twenty-first-century Christians, but were readily accepted in the sixteenth century when Ignatius wrote: "It is my will to conquer all infidel lands. Therefore, whoever wishes to join with me in this enterprise must be content with the same food, drink, clothing, etc. as mine. So, too, he must work with me by day and watch with me by night, etc., that as he has had a share in the toil with me, afterwards he may share in the victory with me."

Now you have to make allowance for the exclusion of women in this address and for the Crusade-like campaign to get those "infidels." Focus instead on those "with me" expressions, notice the hard conditions to which the leader is willing to expose himself and the expectation he has that his followers will be willing to face the same hardships for the good of the hypothetical "cause" entrusted to the leader by God.

Next Ignatius invites the person at prayer to "Consider what the answer of good subjects ought to be to a king so generous and noble-minded, and consequently, if anyone would refuse the invitation of such a king, how justly he would deserve to be condemned by the whole world, and looked upon as an ignoble knight."

Then there is a second part to this meditation where Ignatius introduces you to Christ the King. Ignatius writes:

If such a summons of an earthly king to his subjects deserves our attention, how much more worthy of consideration is Christ our Lord. The Eternal King, before whom is assembled the whole world. To all his summons goes forth, and to each one in particular he addresses the words: "It is my will to conquer the whole world and all my enemies, and thus to enter into the glory of my Father. Therefore, whoever wishes to join me in this enterprise must be willing to labor with me, that by following me in suffering, he may follow me in glory."

Again it is addressed to men only; again the references to "with me." Again, the military mentality. Forget that for the moment and listen again to Ignatius: "Consider that all persons who have judgment and reason will offer themselves entirely for this work."

And then Ignatius proposes what Jesuits call "the magis." He writes:

Those who wish to give greater proof of their love, and to distinguish themselves in the service of the Eternal King and the Lord of all, will not only offer themselves entirely for the work, but will act against their sensuality and carnal and worldly love, and make offerings of greater value and of more importance in words such as these: "Eternal Lord of all things, in the presence of Thy infinite goodness, and of Thy glorious mother, and of all the saints of Thy heavenly court, this is the offering of myself which I make with Thy favor and help. I protest that it is my earnest desire and my deliberate choice, provided only that it I for Thy greater service and praise, to imitate Thee in bearing all wrongs and all abuse and all poverty, both actual and spiritual, should Thy most holy majesty deign to choose and admit me to such a state and way of life."

The words and imagination of Ignatius of Loyola contribute to our answer to that second question I raised earlier—what kind of a king might Jesus have considered himself to be? He was a calling leader, an inviting leader, a leader on a mission, a leader in need of help.

And to our third question for purposes of this homily—how should we view ourselves and conduct ourselves as followers of Christ the King?—there is no better response than the one you just heard in the prayer Ignatius would have you say, "Eternal Lord of all things . . . this is the offering that I wish to make of myself." Go ahead, make your own offering, in your own words.

And if you happen not to be inclined at this moment to make such a prayer, to make such an offering, ask yourself why. Could it be that you don't see Christ as a leader king asking for help?

Could it be that you don't understand the nature of his campaign, the urgency of his cause?

The Church wants us all to give some thought on this Feast of Christ the King to the fact that Christ was and is our king. If the trappings of royalty put us off, notice that he never put the trappings of royalty on! He simply presented himself to us as a leader, an attractive leader, with a cause and an invitation. It is a standing invitation. Respond whenever you like. But respond in the language of love and loyalty and remember if you are willing to share in the work with him, you will surely share in the glory!